# THE REAL FOUNDERS
## OF
# NEW ENGLAND

D1557795

PERILS OF THE SEA

From "Theatrum Orbis Terrarum" by Ortelius, 1579

# THE REAL FOUNDERS
## OF
# NEW ENGLAND

Stories of Their Life Along the Coast
1602–1628

BY

CHARLES KNOWLES BOLTON

CLEARFIELD

Originally Published
Boston, 1929


Reprinted
Genealogical Publishing Co., Inc.
Baltimore, Maryland
1974

Reprinted for
Clearfield Company, Inc. by
Genealogical Publishing Co., Inc.
Baltimore, Maryland
1994, 2004


Library of Congress Catalogue Card Number 74-467
International Standard Book Number 0-8063-0614-9


Made in the United States of America

TO MY GRANDSONS
STANWOOD KNOWLES BOLTON, JUNIOR
AND EDMUND ARNOLD BOLTON
WHO ARE REDISCOVERING THIS
OUR NEW ENGLAND

# PREFACE

THE reader of works relating to New England history soon discovers that the period between the voyage of Gosnold in 1602 and the coming of the Puritans in 1628 and 1630 is passed over with very little more than a reference to two or three of the chief explorers. The material for this period, except for Plymouth, proves to be very meagre. But there is something of fact and romance in these years that may still be recorded.

While it is no longer fashionable to try to divide history into sections, the bounds of which are set by the accidents of war, or by the coming and going of rulers, it is, however, still the vogue, I fear, to assert that History began, as far as New England is concerned, either in 1620 at Plymouth or in 1630 at Boston. The record, whether Indian or English, should, it seems to me, be looked upon as a continuous inter-relation of events. Governor Bradford in August, 1627, stated that the subjects of Queen Elizabeth began to navigate and plant in these lands "well nigh forty years ago." Those who are so constituted that they must begin history with a date might well choose 1587 as a convenient starting point for our story.

These pages (Chapter II) were begun in St. Ives, Cornwall, as I sat looking out upon the fishing boats drawn up along the edge of the quaint gray harbor and half hidden by a cloud of white sea gulls. Chapters III-VII were written in the walled garden of The Fisherman's Retreat, Marlow-on-Thames, with a riot of flowers about me, a large map of our Boston at my feet, and the roar of the distant weir in my ears. Chapter I was written at the British Museum.

I am grateful to Colonel Charles E. Banks for sharing with me unpublished researches in this field, as well as for constant advice; also to Mr. Albert Matthews, Mr. Allen Chamberlain, Dr. Frank A. Gardner, Mr. Emerson Rice, Miss Carrie M. Dodge, and Mr. Alexander Corbett for helpful suggestions. Mr. Worthington C. Ford and Mr. Julius H. Tuttle have responded with patience to my numerous queries.

Mrs. Bolton has drawn or redrawn many of the pictures, and Miss Marjorie Crandall has helped me with the maps. Miss Margaret A. Dodge has worked upon the index. The Massachusetts Historical Society has generously permitted the use of a number of illustrations taken from its edition of Bradford's History.

C. K. B.

*Pound Hill Place*,
*Shirley, July, 1929.*

# CONTENTS

# ILLUSTRATIONS

## CHAPTER IV

## CHAPTER V

CHAPTER IX

# THE REAL FOUNDERS
## OF
# NEW ENGLAND

# I

## THE INDIAN AND THE COD

FOLLOWING a long period of geological history, which included the ice age, Massachusetts Bay began to take on its present outlines. The Merrimac River no longer turned south at Lowell and flowed through Winchester and Cambridge to enter Dorchester Bay at South Boston, but it was carving out its path to Newburyport as we now know it. Vegetation had obliterated the ice scourings except for surface boulders, and wild animals as well as birds gave life to the picture.

Here dwelt the Indians whose ancestors must have been familiar to the Icelandic voyagers, as well as to the earliest French and English cod fishers. It seems to be generally agreed that the Algonquin tribe of red men held the New England coast for the whole period of exploration by Europeans. They were an all powerful factor in colonization enterprises, for they defeated every attempt at permanent settlement from the days of the Norsemen until the pestilence of 1616–19, which weakened their power to resist incursion. At the very outset there was bloodshed. They were by temperament children, fond of red cloth and bright knives. But they were agile and hardy, so that every visitor had reason to fear them.

All the early explorers speak of the savages on the New England coast, their good stature and their volatile temper. Verrazano, the Florentine corsair and explorer, who in 1524 was one of the first of modern continentals to skirt our coast, saw at or near the site of the present Newport and in Maine savages who used iron and copper, and daubed their faces with color. They came out to the ship in canoes made of hollowed logs. Some were friendly and others hostile.

Gabriel Archer, who came over with Gosnold in 1602, wrote of a later generation of these same Indians. They came to him in a shallop with sail and oars. They were naked save for deer skins about the shoulders and near the waists seal skins fashioned like trousers. Their leader wore a waistcoat of black, a pair of breeches, cloth stockings, shoes, and hat — evidence of previous visits to the coast by Europeans. They used "divers Christian words," and were proficient in the use of a piece of chalk to sketch the harbors. Archer called them swart in color, their hair worn long and gathered in a knot behind. Their bodies were strong, well proportioned and daubed with paint. The women were both clean and straight, with countenances "sweet and pleasant." They "would not," said Archer, "admit of any immodest touch."

Smith, with a larger knowledge of the savages, stated that the Massachusetts Indians "have diverse Townes and people belonging; and by their relations

and descriptions, more than 20 severall Habitations
and Rivers that stretch themselves farre up into the
Countrey, even to the borders of diverse great Lakes,
where they kill and take most of their Bevers and
Otters."

To the north were many Indian tribes, chief of
which were the Bashabes of Penobscot, who sometimes warred with the Massachusetts but never came
by sea as far as Cape Cod where the Chawum Indians
lived.

The Rev. William Morrell, who in 1623 lived at
Wessagusset (Weymouth) for many months in close
contact with the Indians, and was our first poet in
New England, speaks with discernment although in
halting verse:

> No former friendship they in minde retaine,
> If you offend once, or your love detaine:
> They're wondrous cruell, strangely base and vile,
> Quickly displeasd, and hardly reconcild;
> Stately and great, as read in Rules of state;
> Incensd, not caring what they perpetrate.
> Whose hayre is cut with greeces, yet a locke
> Is left; the left side bound up in a knott:
> Their males small labour but great pleasure know,
> Who nimbly and expertly draw the bow;
> Traind up to suffer cruell heat and cold,
> Or what attempt so ere may make them bold;
> Of body straight, tall, strong, mantled in skin
> Of Deare or Bever, with the hayre-side in;
> An Otter skin their right armes doth keepe warme,
> To keepe them fit for use, and free from harme;
> A Girdle set with formes of birds or beasts,
> Begirts their waste, which gentle gives them ease.

# New-England.

## OR

# A BRIEFE
# ENARRATION
## OF THE AYRE,

Earth, Water, Fiſh and
Fowles of that Country.

### WITH

# A DESCRIPTION
of the Natures, Orders, Habits,
and Religion of the *Natiues*;

### IN

Latine and Engliſh Verſe.

*Sat brevè, ſi ſat benè.*

---

*LONDON,*
Imprinted by *I. D.*
1 6 2 5.

TITLE PAGE OF MORRELL'S BOOK

And of the women:

> Of comely formes, not blacke, nor very faire:
> Whose beautie is a beauteous blacke laid on
> Their paler cheeke, which they most doat upon:
> For they by Nature are both faire and white,
> Inricht with gracefull presence, and delight;
> Deriding laughter, and all pratling, and
> Of sober aspect, grast with grave command:
> Of man-like courage, stature tall and straight,
> Well nerv'd with hands and fingers small and right.
> Their slender fingers on a grassie twyne,
> Make well form'd Baskets wrought with art and lyne;
> A kind of Arras, or Straw-hangings, wrought
> With divers formes, and colours, all about.
> These gentle pleasures, their fine fingers fit,
> Which Nature seem'd to frame rather to sit;
> Rare Stories, Princes, people, Kingdomes, Towers,
> In curious finger-worke, or Parchment flowers:
> Yet are these hands to labours all intent,
> And what so ere without doores, give content.
> These hands doe digge the earth, and in it lay
> Their faire choyce Corne, and take the weeds away
> As they doe grow, raysing with earth each hill,
> As *Ceres* prospers to support it still.
> Thus all worke-women doe, whilst men in play,
> In hunting, Armes, and pleasures, end the day.[1]

When the whites began to form settlements on the New England coast they encountered in Maine the Abnaki Confederacy of Indians (also called Tarrantines), and on both sides of the Piscataqua the Pennacooks, whose sachem Wannalancet was to become famous in King Philip's War. Around the Bay were the Massachusetts Indians, strong in 1602 but nearly

[1] Governor Bradford and Thomas Morton also wrote verse in New England before the founding of Boston.

annihilated by the plague of 1616. The New Plymouth territory belonged to the Wampanoags as far as the Cape Cod Canal at Bourne; their sachem Massasoit became a friend of the Pilgrims. Subject neighbors on the Cape were called the Nausets, and their descendants are still at Mashpee and Gay Head, Martha's Vineyard. The Massachusetts Indians and their northern and southern neighbors

*figure des sauvages almouchicois*

lost heavily in the plague. Indeed the planters and fishermen, instead of facing 30,000 Indians as Gosnold did, had less than 8,000 against them, all belonging to the Algonquin family, a gentler breed than the Mohawks west of the Connecticut.

The red men were cruel and temperamental but not wholly uncivilized, for they built houses and forts; those to the north of Cape Ann made canoes of birch bark and those to the southward fashioned boats from hollowed logs. They had gardens in which grew beans, pumpkins, squashes, and artichokes as well as tobacco. Each family produced from 20 to 60 bushels of unshelled corn in a season on a well-tilled and weeded acre. In fertilizing their ground, in preparing their food for winter use, and in cooking they could teach the old planters much that was useful. They knew the value of varieties of wood, and they could strike fire. In November of each year they burned the forest underbrush and made travel through the woods possible.

Thus equipped they rendered service to the new civilization, but they never ceased to be a menace. They remained by nature nomadic, and meeting a settled population they too readily assimilated the vices of those pioneer times.

Captain John Smith, in his Description of New England, speaks of explorations by Gosnold, Weymouth, and Popham, adding: "But for divers others that *long before* and since have ranged those parts . . I must entreat them pardon me for omitting them." It is possible that his mind was not clear as to who ranged these parts during the century before he lived.[1] Smith must have been familiar, however, with Gabriel Archer's statement that on this coast in 1602 Gosnold met with a savage who "wore a waist coat of black work, a pair of breeches, cloth stockings, hat and band; one or two more had also a few things made by some Christians." Archer adds that the savages spoke "divers Christian words." This takes us back into the previous century, but how far back we may safely go is quite another question.

Certainly from time beyond the memory of Captain Smith ships had come from Europe to catch and cure fish for the market at home.[2] For this reason the very practical Smith laid great stress on this industry. He writes:

"In March, April, May, and halfe Iune, here is Cod in abundance; in May, Iune, Iuly, and August Mullet and Sturgion; whose roes doe make Caviare and Puttargo. Herring, if any desire them, I have taken many out of the bellies of Cod, some in nets; but the Salvages compare their store in the Sea, to the haires of their heads: and surely there are an incredible abundance upon this Coast. In the end of August, September, October, and November, you have Cod againe to make Cor fish,[3] or Poore Iohn:[4] and each hundred is as good as two or three hundred in the *New-found Land.* So that halfe the labour in hooking, splitting, and turning, is saved: and you may have your fish at what Market you will, before they can have any in *New-found Land:* where

---

[1] Allan Forbes in his "France and New England," volume 3, page xiii, speaks of a captain from Dieppe, with a pilot from Rouen, on our coast in 1506.

[2] As early as the year 1517 there were fifty French, Spanish and Portuguese fishing ships on the coast. — Palfrey, volume 1, page 65.

[3] Cod never disembowelled but thoroughly salted in pickle and packed without drying.

[4] Salted and dried hake.

their fishing is chiefly but in Iune and Iuly: whereas it is heere
in March, April, May, September, October, and November, as
is said. So that by reason of this plantation, the Marchants may
have fraught both out and home: which yeelds an advantage
worth consideration.

"The Mullets heere are in that abundance, you may take them
with nets, sometimes by hundreds, where at *Cape blank* they hooke

A View of a Stage. also ye manner of Fishing for, Curing & Drying of Cod
at NEW FOUND LAND. A. The Habit of the Fishermen. B. The Line. C. They
manner of Fishing. D. The Dressers of the Fish. E. The Trough into which
they throw the Cod when dressed. F. Salt Boxes. G. The manner of carrying the Cod. H. The Cleansing of the Cod. I. A Press to extract the Oyl
from the Cods Livers. K. A Cask to receive the Water and Blood that comes
from the Livers. L. another Cask to receive the Oyl. M. The manner of
drying the Cod.

them; yet those but one foot and a halfe in length; these two, three, or foure, as oft I have measured: much Salmon some have found up the Rivers, as they have passed: and heer the ayre is so temperate, as all these at any time may well be preserved.

"Now, young boyes and girles Salvages, or any other, be they never such idlers, may turne, carry, and return fish, without either shame or any great paine: hee is very idle that is past twelve yeares of age and cannot doe so much: and she is very olde, that cannot spin a thred to make engines to catch them."

At the time of the voyage of Gosnold in 1602, and even before his coming to the New England coast, we see the harbors and rivers alive with shipping. Whitbourne in his description of Newfoundland says that 250 vessels came to the coast in the year 1615. From very early in the spring until late in the fall fleets of fishing ships were in New England waters. Each island that possessed a protected cove had its rude house where the fishermen slept, ate, and kept their possessions. There were also platforms called stages where the fishes were split, cleaned and dried. Near these stages were warehouses where the dried or pickled fish were stored, and there were hogsheads of salt (as well as casks of liquor). Presses for extracting oil from the livers of the cod, and instruments for fishing, repair of boats and sails, all served their part in the business of fishing.[1]

John Josselyn's adventures in New England are described[2] with a touch of malice, but his picture of life on the Maine coast is vivid:

[1] After four centuries of cod fishing off Monhegan and Cape Cod it is still not very unusual, I am told by Mr. Edward Stanwood of Provincetown, for fishermen to take a cod weighing from 75 to 100 pounds.

[2] Mass. Hist. Soc. Coll., third series, volume 3, page 351.

"To every Shallop belong four fishermen, a Master
or Steersman, a midship-man, and a Foremastman,
and a shore man who washes it out of the salt, and
dries it upon hurdles pitcht upon stakes breast high
and tends their Cookery; these often get in one voyage Eight or Nine pound a man for their shares, but
it doth some of them little good, for the Merchant to
increase his gains by putting off his Commodity in
the midst of their voyages, and at the end thereof
comes in with a walking Tavern, a Bark laden with
the Legitimate bloud of the rich grape, which they
bring from *Phial* (Fayal), *Madera, Canaries,* with
*Brandy, Rhum,* the *Barbadoes strong-water,* and *Tobacco,* coming ashore he gives them a Taster or two,
which so charms them, that for no perswasions that
their imployers can use will they go out to Sea, although fair and seasonable weather, for two or three
days, nay sometimes a whole week till they are
wearied with drinking, taking ashore two or three
Hogsheads of *Wine* and *Rhum* to drink off when the
Merchant is gone.  If a man of quality chance to
come where they are roystering and gulling in *Wine*
with a dear felicity, he must be sociable and *Roly-
poly* with them, taking off their liberal cups as freely,
or else be gone, which is best for him, for when *Wine*
in their guts is at full Tide, they quarrel, fight and
do one another mischief, which is the conclusion of
their drunken compotations.  When the day of pay-
ment comes, they may justly complain of their costly
sin of drunkenness, for their shares will do no more
than pay the reckoning; if they save a Kental or two

to buy shooes and stockins, shirts and wastcoats with, 'tis well, other-wayes they must enter into the Merchants books for such things as they stand in need off, becoming thereby the Merchants slaves, & when it riseth to a big sum are constrained to mortgage their plantation if they have any, the Merchant when the time is expired is sure to seize upon their plantation and stock of Cattle, turning them out of house and home, poor Creatures, to look out for a new habitation in some remote place where they begin the world again."

On the larger rivers were trading posts where men engaged in barter for furs of the beaver, the bear, and the fox. The honest merchant had cloth, knives, hatchets and such like articles to exchange for pelts. But the more unscrupulous traders, such as Walter Bagnall at Richmond Island, Thomas Purchase at Pejepscot, and Edward Astley on the Penobscot, are said to have sold powder and shot, rapier blades (for arrow tips), and old guns to enrich themselves quickly, not scrupling to cheat the Indians.

THOMAS PURCHES

At these trading posts and fishing stages the venturesome sailors of the English seacoast met, gambled, drank strong liquor, quarreled, did business in fish and fur, as well as in the buying and selling of the terms of indentured servants. There was, no doubt, immorality as was charged against Astley, and roguery such as that which stirred the Indians to take Bagnall's life. The work was hard and rough, but the men were tolerant of one another. They may not have found favor with the saints but — to parody a saying of James Savage in criticizing the first minister of Boston — neither could some of the acts of bigotry of the leaders of the Massachusetts Bay prove acceptable to gentlemen.

EDWARD ASTLEY

Richmond Island, off Cape Elizabeth, is a good example of a fishing and trading post. It seems to have been named for George Richmond of Bandon Bridge in old Ireland, who may have been there very early; but he is a shadowy figure. John Burgess had a house there at the time of his death in 1627. His widow was named Bray, and it is possible that her family, later well known at Kittery, had early connection with the place. In 1628 Walter Bagnall came up from Merrymount in the Bay and began business. He was a shrewd but ruthless man, and if he brought with him some of the Merrymount party they were given to drinking and gambling. But Bagnall kept his head and amassed a fortune by exchanging trinkets and liquor for beaver skins. Morton of Merrymount heard that he had at one time property valued at £1,000, then a large sum. Ships were in and out of his harbor, and the usual boisterous ele-

ment was always in evidence. Indians came and
went, or settled down to work for Bagnall and received in return hard usage and strong drink.

MAP OF RICHMOND ISLAND

Bagnall kept a considerable sum of money at the
post, and buried it in a quart earthen pot about a
foot below the surface of the earth and about four
rods from the shore. His buildings were a few feet
away. In 1854 the land was ploughed, and on May
11th of the next year the plough going deeper turned
up the pot which was filled with caked earth. The
bottom held many coins, the silver on one side, the
gold sovereigns and half sovereigns on the other side
with a man's signet ring in the centre. The 31 pieces
of silver were discolored but the 21 gold coins were

fresh and clear. They ranged from Queen Elizabeth's time down to 1625.[1] Bagnall was killed 3 October, 1631,[2] by Indians led by Sagamore Squidraket, or Scitterygusset, who plundered his warehouse, killed his associate, and burned his buildings. The pot seems to have been his, and it contained a riddle of the heart not to be looked for amid such surroundings. The ring referred to has engraved upon it two united hearts with the words "United hearts[3] Death only Partes," and the initials "G. V." The uncommon initial "V" at once points to the Vines family. Richard Vines was a distinguished explorer and trader on the coast as early as 1616, and was of a generation before that to which Bagnall belonged. This ring could tell of events which may have had much to do with the career of a man who lived for years on a bleak island off the New England coast.

WALTER BAGNALL'S RING

[1] Burrage's Beginnings, 1914, page 200. Mass. Hist. Soc. Proc., May, 1857, page 183. Trelawny Papers.

[2] The day of the month is 10 days earlier in all cases than our reckoning, which would be 13 October, 1631. The new year began 25 March, March being the first month of the year.

[3] Instead of the word "hearts" the engraver has drawn two hearts united.

We get occasional glimpses of the tragedy that dogs those who go down to the sea in ships. In March, 1623–24, the pinnace *Little James* went up from Plymouth to Pemaquid for fish. She was moored to the shore by passing a rope around a boulder. The 10th of April a great storm arose, and such waves as had never been seen before traversed the harbor. The rope worked loose and the *Little James* went on the rocks. She then slid into deep water and turned over, carrying her master down. As she went her main yard crushed a boat and threw six or seven men into the sea. Two were drowned. Most of her boats were sunk and her cargo ruined. Other ships from England rode out the storm.

JOHN WYNTER

Since much of the fishing went on in February, March, and April, the life was hard.[1] John Winter at Richmond Island in 1635 tells of a boat that set out with her usual complement of three men. They did not return. He went in search and found their bodies floating in the icy water. The sail had overturned the boat which the men righted, but they lacked the strength or the means to bail her out.

[1] Christopher Levett (Baxter), page 64.

## II

## VISITORS TO THE COAST, 1602–1622

LIFE in the Massachusetts Bay did not begin with Captain Gosnold's voyage in 1602. His story, however, is of an attempt to found a colony in New England, rather than the usual narrative of exploration or fishing.

Bartholomew Gosnold set sail from Falmouth in Cornwall 26 March, 1602, with two small ships, the *Concord* and the *Dartmouth*. Thirty-two persons were on board, of whom eight were mariners and sailors. On the 14th of May, after many soundings and meeting with floating seaweed and wood, they sighted land to the north of them and found a great rock which they called Savage Rock, because the red men first showed themselves there. This was probably off York Beach.[1] Cruising southward, Gosnold on the 15th sighted land which he thought an island but found to be a cape. Having taken a great store of codfish he named the place Cape Cod. He did not go into Massachusetts Bay.[2]

The explorers visited islands south of the Cape, on one of which they found gooseberry, whortleberry and raspberry bushes, with many varieties of wild fowl and birds. They named this island Martha's Vineyard. The Indians came to visit them, friendly

[1] But the Salvidge Isles were off Cape Ann.
[2] But strictly speaking "Massachusetts Bay" in those days meant Boston Harbor only.

but thievish, bringing deer skins, copper and tobacco for barter.

Sailing on, Gosnold came to a chain of four small islands at the entrance to Buzzard's Bay and off Wood's Hole. He named the outer island Elizabeth's Isle. It is now called Cuttyhunk. Here he decided to settle his colony, and on the 28th (old style) selected a rocky islet (near the present lighthouse), covering an acre of cedar-clad land, in a fresh-water pond, amid sassafras, hawthorn and honeysuckle. On the rocks were countless little turtles some of which, seen by Gosnold, may still be dreaming away their days in the mud at the bottom of the pond. Groves of oak, ash, beech, walnut and cedar offered shade and firewood. Here Gosnold's men built a fort and planted peas.

MAP OF CUTTYHUNK

Meanwhile all were active, some in gathering sassafras root, then held in great esteem as a medicine, others in making a flat-bottomed punt for crossing their pond, while Captain Gosnold explored the shore of the mainland.

Early in June the stockade was completed and the friendly Indians were given a banquet of English cooked food, crabs, fish, ground nuts and beer. The savages ate freely of strong mustard and set the sailors laughing over their grimaces. The sailors stuffed themselves with the bellies of dog-fish and gave the savages an exhibition of pain after meat.

From the narrative written by Gabriel Archer, one of the company, we can see savages decked in straw hats and cast-off garments, enacting the part of timid yet kindly children, generous and fierce by turns, whose good will was necessary for the well being of the little colony.

Work on a storehouse was pushed rapidly while the Captain went away to get cedar logs. During his absence a foraging sailor was hit by an arrow and this brought on a panic. Provisions ran short. Archer ordered his men to gather "sorrel pottage" and ground nuts, such as acorns. With these and tobacco the men kept up their strength. On the 12th they heard the Captain's shout which "made such music as sweeter never came unto poor men."

With provision made for every need and with a summer before them, the future looked bright. Nevertheless, the division of stores, part for the returning crew and part for the remaining planters, aroused suspicion of unfair play, and one by one the planters came to a decision not to be left behind. Gosnold ordered food and fuel to be gathered for the return voyage, and the ships set sail on the 18th of June. They dropped anchor on July 23d at Exmouth, with the last loaf of bread and the last drop of water gone. Thus ended Gosnold's colony. With forceful leadership New England would have been settled before Virginia.

Already the West of England was much awake to profit from trade across the Atlantic. The merchants of Bristol fitted out the *Speedwell,* 50 tons, and the bark *Discoverer,* 26 tons. They gave the command to an experienced navigator, Martin Pring. Edmund Jones went as mate, with Robert Salterne as agent or business manager. William Browne was placed in command of the bark, with Samuel Kirkland as his mate. The larger ship carried 30 men and boys, the smaller had on board 13 persons. They took a curious cargo for barter: stockings and shoes, saws, pickaxes, spades and hatchets, hooks, knives, "sizzers," nails and fishhooks, as well as bugles. For the fair sex they carried looking-glasses, thimbles, needles and thread.

The ships put forth 20 March, 1602–03, from "Kingrode," and fell down to Milford Haven in Wales, where they heard of the death of Queen Elizabeth. This great event did not deter the commander, for he set sail 10 April, 1603, sighted the Azores, and came at last to several small islands on the New England coast in latitude 43°, somewhere off the Penobscot. This was in June. Passing on to the main land they found fires where people had been, as well as deer, wolves, foxes and dogs.[1]

Sassafras, however, they could not find, and so set sail to the southward and entered a great gulf which, says Pring, Captain Gosnold had overshot the year before. They followed the north side of Massachusetts Bay, seeing Indians at places on the shore which we now call Salem, Marblehead and Lynn. Still unsatisfied in their expectation they left this region, and "sailed over," coming to anchor on the south side, in latitude 41 degrees "and odde minutes."

Here they found a pleasant harbor, and beside it a hill which they called Mount Aldworth. This seems clearly to be Plymouth. They at once built a small barricade "to keep diligent watch and ward in while working in the wood." The soil was sandy and the sassafras, whose medicinal qualities men so much appreciated, was abundant. Indians, protected by brass plates, and armed with witch hazel bows, carrying yard-long feathered arrows, came to them in groups of from 10 to 60. They ate with the sailors, sharing beans, peas and fish. After they had eaten their fill the sailors played the "Gitterne" for the red men to dance.

While the hold of the *Discoverer* was being loaded with sassafras, two great mastiffs named "Foole" and

[1] The dog was domesticated throughout the length and breadth of America in prehistoric times. — C. C. Willoughby.

"Gallant" played with the Indians, but aroused their fear. Thoughtless men for sport set the dogs on the natives and stirred them to anger.

At the end of July the *Discoverer* was sent home, laden with sassafras. The men who gathered it had slept in the woods and depended for protection as much upon the dogs as upon their firearms. The departure of part of the company in the smaller vessel may have given the red men courage to attempt to force the other workers out of the country; or there may have been fresh cause of irritation. In any case, the Indians set fire to the undergrowth in the woods early in August. No serious damage was done but Pring took alarm and decided to return to England.

Two years later (1605) the Earl of Southampton joined with his son-in-law, Lord Arundell of Wardour, and Sir Ferdinando Gorges to fit out a ship called the *Archangel*. The command was given to Captain George Weymouth. After an uneventful voyage from Ratcliffe on the Thames, Weymouth reached Nantucket on May 14th and sailed northward, reaching Monhegan May 18th. With him came a Roman Catholic priest, perhaps with missions in mind.

He explored a large river in Maine, did a good business in barter with the Indians and sailed away on June 16th, arriving at Dartmouth on July 18th. His voyage was described by James Rosier, who had been with Gosnold in 1602. The narrative aroused Sir John Popham and Gorges to the possibilities of

the New England coast.  Letters patent of James I
in 1606 gave the territory between 38° and 44° north
latitude (Cape May to Cape Sable) to the adventurers of the south and west of England.

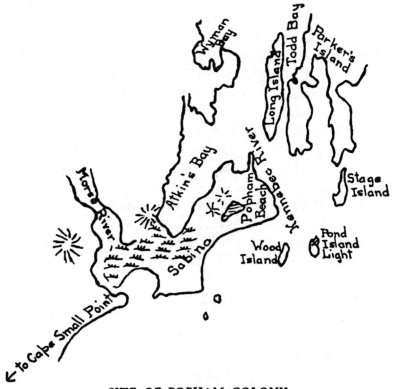

SITE OF POPHAM COLONY

No event in New England history has been
so much the centre of stormy controversy as the
Popham colony, sometimes called the earliest attempt at true colonization in New England.  In

June, 1607, they sailed from Plymouth in the *Gift of God,* with a sister ship, the *Mary and John,* under command of Raleigh Gilbert. Chief Justice Sir John Popham, a great figure in England at the time, was their backer. They sighted land 27 July, 1607 (at 43° 40″), near Cape Elizabeth and soon came to Damariscove, Wood Island, and Outer Heron. They then passed Seguin and "made their plantation" at Hunnewell's Point, called by the Indians Sabino.[1] Some say that trial was first made at Parker's Island and Stage Island.

On August 20th they entrenched, and at once began to construct Fort St. George and a storehouse. They also set to work on a pinnace for exploring the coast and rivers. Captain Gilbert meanwhile sailed as far south as Casco Bay. The Hon. James W. Patterson, a revered historian who still lives at Wiscasset, spoke of this "church colony on the peninsula of Sabino" as "hallowed ground." By December, 1607, some 45 settlers had left the colony; and when Captain Richard Davies arrived from England in the spring of 1608 he found that the men had endured a severe winter, and were discontented. Captain Popham was dead and Gilbert wished to go home to claim an estate. The colony came to an end in October, but the controversy over the significance of the undertaking still survives.[2]

[1] At the mouth of the Kennebec, then known as the Sagadahoc. Referred to in 1609 as "the colonies of Exceter and Plymou'" (Brown's Genesis, page 259).

[2] "Rootes and Garden hearbs and some old walles" could still be seen in 1660, said Maverick.

When the Devonshire men near Popham Beach abandoned their colony in the fall of 1608, it is said (as well as denied) that a few settlers went to Pemaquid instead of returning to England. The statement by James Davies, "Wherefore then *all* ymbarqued," is not to be taken as exact since several, seeing the approaching end of the experiment, may have sought new quarters. It seems to me possible that a Captain Damerill was of Popham's colony — his is a Devon name — and that he saw the great strategic value of the neighboring island off Cape Newagen, now known as Damariscove. It has the best small landlocked harbor on the coast and it was heavily wooded. Here he or his servants would seem to have been when Captain John Smith put into the cove in 1614, and described it as "Damerils Iles." This name must have been generally accepted along the coast, for Phinehas Pratt in 1622 refers to Damoralls Cove, the Virginians in 1625 called it Dambrells Cove, the Massachusetts Colonial Records in 1632 speak of Damerills Cove, and John Parker lived at Dammarill's Cove in 1645. As late as 1686 John Sellman was at Dambrells Cove. From 1608 onward the Virginians had gone there for fish.[1]

No doubt many of the scores of fishing vessels that came to the coast each season put into the Cove for water, liquor, salt and fuel. A record of the recorded voyages to the fishing grounds near Pemaquid, Monhegan and Damerill's Cove shows that the neighborhood was by no means isolated or destitute of com-

[1] J. A. Poor's Vindication of Gorges, 1862, page 47.

pany.  There is evidence that when ships arrived
from Spain with casks of wine the men were merry
enough.

| | |
|---|---|
| 1607–16. | Ships each year from England.[1] |
| 1608. | Captain Davies.  Henry Hudson searching for a north-west passage saw a mermaid at sea. |
| 1609– | Virginia traders came each year for fish. |
| | Henry Hudson at Mt. Desert in the *Half Moon*. |
| 1610. | Captain Samuel Argall to Sagadahoc and Cape Cod. |
| 1611. | Biencourt and Biard visited the ruins of George Popham's colony. |
| 1611–12. | Captain Edward Harlow or Harley along the coast. |
| 1614. | Captain John Smith's voyage to New England. |
| | Sir Francis Popham's ships at Pemaquid where they had come for "many years." |
| 1614–20. | "80 ships in the trade." |
| 1615. | Captain Thomas Dermer or Dormer.  Details not known. |
| 1615–16. | Four good ships came. |
| | Sir Richard Hawkins wintered at Monhegan? |
| 1616. | Eight ships from England, R. Vines in command of one?[1] |
| 1616–17. | Richard Vines at Saco all this winter or the next. |
| 1618–20. | Trade described by Smith. |
| 1618–19. | Captain Edward Rocroft's crew at Monhegan. |
| 1619. | Captain Dermer sailed along the coast. |

RICHARD VINES

Damerill had a storehouse at the Cove, stages for
drying fish, repair shops, and huts, for he kept men
on the island the year round.  The race across the

---

[1] A. Brown's Genesis, page 779.

Atlantic each winter from the channel ports meant that the first to arrive appropriated every uninhabited building to be seen, and occupied it or removed the planks to a new site. In this race some ships carried so much sail that they lost their masts or capsized. Damerill could not leave his island unprotected. When Humphrey Damerill, a kinsman of the above Captain, died in the spring of 1654 he left a wife, Sarah, and a son, John. The widow married John Hawkins, a mariner, who in 1657 assigned his interest in Damerill's estate to the son, John. The inventory dated 27 April, 1654, shows a large furnished house, with "2 sea plotts & a sea booke" among its contents. There was also a bark, the *Sea Flower,* of which Damerill was commander; it was valued at £140. Rev. H. O. Thayer in the Maine Historical Society Collections, second series, volume 6, page 80, says that Damerill's heirs claimed part of the island. This I have not been able to verify.

The period of New England history into which we are about to enter is singularly destitute of informal documentary evidence, and yet there is much to be said for the theory that the white man from now on kept a foothold on the coast. Colonel Banks writes:

"The basic charter of King James, dated 3 Nov., 1620, in favor of the Northern Company (The Plymouth Council) asserts as a reason for granting it that *already* there were settlements in that region 'by our subjects,' etc. As this was prior to the landing of the 'Forefathers' on Cape Cod and the establishment of the Pilgrim colony, it is clear that this sentence has

no relation to them, as they had not left England
when the charter was preparing.

"Capt. John Smith gives the story of annual fleets
coming to Monhegan and Damariscove. Consider
what this suggests. They cured their catches ashore
and that implies buildings, flakes, etc., and no one
supposes that the hundreds of fishermen remained in
the cramped fo'castles of these small craft when they
could live comfortably ashore, get fresh water easily,
enjoy life, and indulge in sports and recreations necessary for existence. I think it quite unassailable to
say that buildings were erected — not mansions —
rough structures where their business could be carried on easily ashore. They knew they were coming
back the following spring of each year, and it does
not require much imagination to picture these structures as storage places for material of which they
would be in constant need. This sort of natural de-
velopment must have gone on to the point of making
these centres of activity, Damariscove and Monhegan, permanent headquarters for their continued use.
We cannot suppose they lived 'from hand to mouth,'
each recurring trip, huddled in small vessels and
making no provision for permanency. That wasn't
like Englishmen then in rivalry with France and
Spain to establish a permanent foothold on the coast.
I think this led by gradual survival to the establishment of winter settlements of men left behind to
guard the property in storage as well as the buildings
which housed them. The Damariscove palisado of
1622, an elaborate affair, was not an outgrowth of the

puny, half starving settlement of Plymouth, almost without houses even in the spring of 1621. It represented much time and labor to erect such a 'fort' — ten feet high, built of logs, etc. The Pilgrims gave no impetus to this undertaking.

"Is there any other evidence of such a permanent settlement or settlements on the Maine coast prior to 1620? What seems to me a significant fact in corroboration is to be found in the settlement undertaken at the mouth of the Saco in 1618. Capt. Edward Rocroft was sent by Gorges in a ship of 200 tons to fish on the well-established fishing grounds. He captured a French bark lying in one of the harbors there, sent her crew in his own ship to England, and retained the bark with a view to winter here. A mutiny occurred and he put the mutineers ashore at Saco, sailing in December for Virginia. What followed seems to me significant — of something important to this theory. *They made their way to Monhegan where they spent the winter.* Why? Because they must have known that it was inhabited. Else why leave the mainland where they could be sure to subsist on game and perhaps with friendly natives to go to an island twenty miles out to sea, where there was no subsistence (game) to be had — unless a settlement existed for the use of the yearly fleet of vessels? I see no answer to this — save one — they knew they could find habitations and people and stores there. Otherwise, it sounds like a fool performance to leave the real source of subsistence on shore to go to a barren island in the winter time."

In 1609 the Earl of Southampton sent an expedition to New England under Captain Edward Harlow, a member of Popham and Gilbert's colony in 1607, which made some corrections in the map of the coast line, proving that Cape Cod was part of the mainland and not an island.[1]  They trapped five savages, lost their lifeboat, and at last got away for England.

The voyage of Captain John Smith in 1614 made an epoch, for his own narrative and map promoted colonization for years to come.  He had been for over two years in Virginia where experience was a hard teacher, and he came to New England with no soft-handed illusions about life in a new world.

"In the moneth of Aprill, 1614," he writes, "with two ships from London I chanced to arrive in New-England, parte of Ameryca, at the Ile of Monahiggan."  While the sailors fished Smith ranged the coast in a small boat, collecting beaver skins.  He found a Popham ship "right against us in the Main," Popham having many years been active there, and 40 leagues to the westward were two French ships, doing a profitable business.

Smith calls the country of the Massachusetts "the Paradise of all those parts"; and continues: "For, heere are many Iles all planted with corne; groves, mulberries, salvage gardens, and good harbors: the Coast is for the most part, high clayie sandie cliffs. The Sea Coast as you passe, shewes you all along

[1] Adriaen Block is said to have sailed as far north as Cape Cod in 1613–14, and perhaps to Nahant Bay.

large corne fields, and great troupes of well proportioned people: but the *French* having remained heere
neere sixe weekes, left nothing for us to take occasion
to examine the inhabitants relations, *viz.* if there be
neer three thousand people upon these Iles; and that
the River doth pearce many daies iourneis the intralles
of that Countrey. We found the people in those parts
verie kinde; but in their furie no lesse valiant. For,
upon a quarrel wee had with one of them, hee onely
with three others crossed the harbor of *Quonahassit*
to certaine rocks whereby wee must passe; and there
let flie their arrowes for our shot, till we were out of
danger."

In 1615 Sir Richard Hawkins came to Pemaquid, and after wintering there explored the coast
toward Virginia. In 1616 eight ships sailed for New
England.

Phinehas Pratt in his Narrative tells us that before
the year 1616/17 a French trading vessel, lying off
Peddock's Island in Boston Harbor, was captured by
the Indians and burned. This is proof, if any were
needed, that fishing fleets put into Massachusetts Bay.

Richard Vines, a very early settler on our shores,
may have come over first with Popham or perhaps
with Weymouth. He had been in the country as
early as 1609 as the trusted agent of Sir Ferdinando
Gorges. It is known that Vines passed the winter of
1616/17 at a sheltered basin called Winter Harbor,
but now known as Biddeford Pool at the mouth of
the Saco River, in order to convince the doubting

friends of Gorges that life on this coast would not be impossible.   It was the period of a pestilence among the Indians, reported by him.[1]   The fancy of one

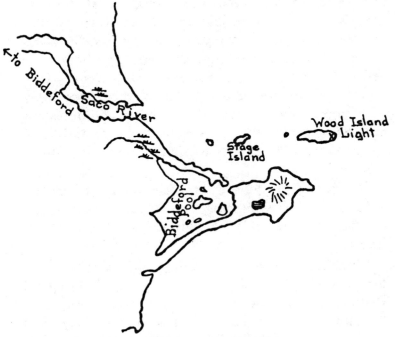

MAP OF BIDDEFORD POOL

writer has pictured his home as a group of "low-walled, clay-plastered, dingy log huts," on the rim of a little harbor.   Here Vines and his associates camped at intervals during the succeeding years until he finally settled down to pass what was left of his life there in the company of Morgan Howell and other

[1] An infectious fever or malignant typhus which nearly destroyed the Massachusetts tribe.   Several explorers commented on this plague.

neighbors. The historian of Saco calls him an ardent Churchman.

Captain Thomas Dermer in the summer of 1619 came down from Monhegan as far as Cape Cod in an open pinnace of five tons. He rescued two Frenchmen, one from the Massachusetts Indians, that had been shipwrecked three years before off Cape Cod. Dermer found many savages covered with sores, and also plantations where all had perished. After being captured and after suffering from fever he arrived safely in Virginia, where he died.

In November, 1620, after long beating about at sea, the *Mayflower,* bound for the Hudson River, ran among shoals southeast of Cape Cod, and fearing trouble after dark put back into Provincetown harbor, as we now call it. The cold and dreary weeks following were given over to exploration of the coast, vividly described by Bradford. By the middle of December they had come upon Plymouth harbor with its safe anchorage, cleared land, a hill, and brook of sweet water. Here they settled, and on the 25th began to erect the first house for common use to receive them and their goods. One hundred and two came over in the ship, and of these fifty-one died this first winter. Whether due to incompetent seamanship, misfortune, or treachery, the Pilgrims had arrived too late in the year for a comfortable beginning of their enterprise.

When these settlers had endured the hardships of their first winter, and had begun to reap the fruits

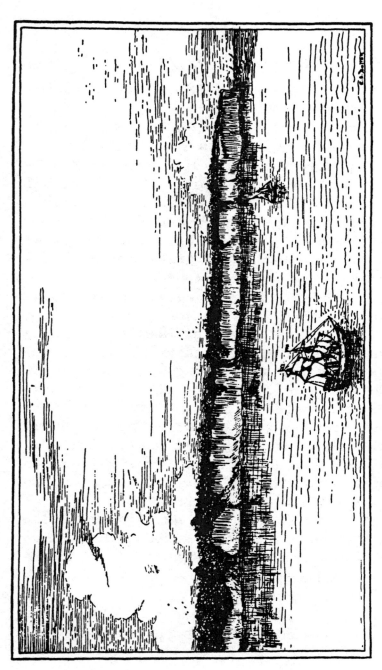

VIEW OF CAPE COD

of their first planting, Myles Standish with nine others and three Indian interpreters came into Massachusetts Bay, arriving at the end of September, 1621.[1] The pestilence had decimated the local Indian tribe, so that Standish found only a few weak, disheartened red men on the shore.

The Plymouth people followed the coast to the rocky point called Squantum, where they found many lobsters which they "made ready" under the cliff. They then talked with Obbatinewat, the local sachem, who said that the raids made annually by the Indians from the Penobscot River so frightened his people that they had no settled homes. Standish then crossed over to Charlestown, as it is now called, stopping on the way at an island off Dorchester — now Thompson's Island — and spent the night in the shallop which rode at anchor. He then marched as far as Mystic Pond in Medford, and saw the grave of Nanepashemet, the famous sachem. The Indians were very timid but at last took heart and carried on a brisk barter in skins. The shallop then returned to Plymouth, having been gone from the 18th to the 22d of September, old style.

In all this period of exploration and fishing it is clear that it was the coast of Maine which attracted the adventurous. Their entry into Massachusetts Bay to obtain water, corn and sassafras had no part in their larger plans. The country which Smith called a paradise was now to claim that attention which led

[1] See Mourt's Relation, page 124.

in time to its domination over all the other settlements on the coast as far north as the boundary of Canada.

It was the English nation which took an active interest in that section of the coast known as New England. Our American ambassador, Mr. Page, looking out on St. Ives harbor in Cornwall, wrote to a friend: "The trouble with the Englishman is that he got great world power too easily. In the times when he exploited the world for his own enrichment there were no other successful exploiters. It became an easy game to him. He organized sea traffic and sea power."

All this may be true, but he who reads of the settling of Virginia and New England must feel that the will to endure privation and danger is very much to the credit of "the successful exploiter."

# III

## SETTLEMENTS, 1622–1625

IF we are to imagine ourselves back in Mr. Blaxton's time we must see the Massachusetts Bay as "the Paradise of all those parts," to use Captain Smith's words. The sheet of water, hemmed in from the open ocean by Cape Ann to the north and the tip of Cape Cod to the south, held many fair islands; some of these were wooded, and others were planted with corn, and described as "salvage gardens." Along the southern side — now known as Barnstable, Plymouth, Weymouth and Quincy — the flats at low tide would seem to the navigators of our day as uninviting, but the small ships of that time, with their shallow draft, found a safe haven at the mouth of tidal streams. The Charles and Mystic rivers were not, apparently, much explored as yet. But Shawmut, barren and dreary as it was, did furnish the best of fresh water, and the fishing fleet must have known its springs.

If we could have skirted the irregular shore of the Bay with a party from Plymouth under Captain Myles Standish in September, 1621, the only smoke rising above the trees would have come from the wigwams of the few Indians who had survived famine and pestilence in these regions.

The line between the land-loving class and the seafarers was more clearly defined then than it is now. The landsman never went to sea if he could avoid it. The sea folk who lived along the English coast from Plymouth in the south to Bristol in the west had a language all their own and a love of rough adventure beyond any of our day. Their keel, said Sir Thomas Overbury, was the emblem of their conscience. Till it be split they never repented. Their ships which sought a passage to Cathay had the fore and main masts square rigged and the mizzen rigged with a lateen sail. Ships of this type and era made leeway terribly fast in a storm, and were too short to ride two ridges of the usual long sea swells at a time. They were, therefore, in constant motion on every day except the calmest.

Besides the crew there was a cook to dress the meat — gammons of bacon, salt fish, pork and stewed mutton packed in crocks — a cooper to care for the casks, and a swabber to scrub the decks and reduce, if possible, the stench of the bilge water. Mr. Chatterton in his life of Captain John Smith pictures ship life in warm weather as extremely unhealthy. The hulls leaked, the food grew musty, and the water lost all its flavor.

In the stories of early New England much is said of the shallop which was carried in parts ready to be put together on reaching land. She was, says Mr. Chatterton, rigged with a fore stay sail (shaped like a jib) and sprit mainsail (a sail whose peak is held out from the mast by a spar), the sail being laced to the mast. Such a craft was useful to explore bays and rivers, and in case of shipwreck she could carry a company of perhaps twenty or thirty persons to safety.

For a century or more after the first voyage of Columbus sailing ships dropped down to the Canaries and there picked up the northeast trades to bear them westward to the West Indies and the American coast. Gosnold in 1602 bore more to the westward, picked up the Azores, and steered a course which brought him to Cape Ann.

It was customary at this time to drop down to the parallel of 43° 15′ (west of Cape Finisterre), and run westward until soundings indicated the Grand Banks. A week or so later Cape Sable appeared to starboard, and in four or five days "The Three Turks Heads" of Mt. Agamenticus (York) showed dead ahead.[1]

A few writers have given us details of the voyage. Two weeks out of port the sea water began to change its color to a cobalt blue and the whole life of the ocean was new. The air became warmer, the water was dotted with little bunches of seaweed — yellow ochre patches, sometimes floating singly but more often in procession, marching over the crested waves. The Rev. Richard Mather calls them a "variety of yellow weeds." For the first half of the journey Mother Carey's chickens hung like little swerving aeroplanes over the water, and tip tilting they turned their white breasts to the sunlight. In the middle of the ocean flying fishes — whole schools of them — shot out of

[1] Colon. Soc. of Mass. Pub., December, 1908, pages 200-201. H. E. Ware.

THE THREE TURKS HEADS
Agamenticu, now York

the swirling sea, skimmed the surface, and splashed below. A stately chambered nautilus sailed proudly by. Slippery arched porpoises played about the ships, and whales spouted frequently as they still used to do a half century ago.

Mather speaks of the stormy petrel or Mother Carey's chicken. He mentions also the playful porpoises, one of which was cut open on the deck and was, he said, "wonderful to us all, and marvellous merry sport, and delightful to our women and children." With salt, pepper and vinegar the flesh proved to be good eating. He refers to the whale, grampus, bonito or Spanish dolphin, mackerel and cod; he also notices a change in the color of the water on approaching land. The appearance of a bird with blue colored feathers attracted his notice.

When the passengers tired of salt fish and salt beef they had, one writer records, "bacon and buttered peas, sometimes buttered bag-pudding made with currants and raisins, with pottage (or soup) of beer[1] and oatmeal, or water pottage, well buttered."

The Rev. Francis Higginson had similar experiences to put down in the Journal of his voyage; and Governor Winthrop tells of social meetings with people from other ships during periods of calm, for ships then rarely sailed alone.

The late Charles Francis Adams, President of the Massachusetts Historical Society, has left us the best

---

[1] Colonel Banks says: "Hogsheads of beer were carried and relied on as antiscorbutic in value; hence coopers (example, John Alden) were a necessary part of the crew to care for the safety of the casks, etc."

MASSACHUSETTS BAY, 1633

account of "the old planters about Boston harbor," and I propose to avail myself of his studies. About the middle of May, 1622, the ship *Sparrow,* sent out by Thomas Weston, a London merchant, reached Damariscove, near Monhegan. Gibbs, the master's mate, with nine other men, including Phinehas Pratt,

*Phinehas Pratt.*

PHINEHAS PRATT

set out in a coasting boat to find a site for a settlement, leaving the crew to fish and make merry round a may-pole. The boat passed the Isles of Shoals, and Cape Ann. It then came into Massachusetts Bay and the men passed four or five days in exploration. They hit upon the centre of the south shore of the Bay, and a rough map of 1633[1] places the spot on land nearly opposite the mouth of the Quincy River "and a little if anything north of it." Here was good anchorage, and an unobstructed view of the harbor through "Hull Gut" — between Hull and Peddock's Island (the modern names). The ground in the neighborhood was rolling country and suited to agriculture, with deep soil. A large mussel bed furnished shellfish, then popular as food but now not much appreciated.

Fresh water was to be had. The site was north of a glacial deposit (Hunt's Hill), now removed,

[1] See Mass. Hist. Soc. Proc., June, 1884.

and the anchorage, now King's Cove, was south
of the hill.[1]

### WESSAGUSSET

| | | |
|---|---|---|
| A. Hough's Neck | C. Great Hill | E. Hunt's Hill |
| B. Germantown | D. Rowe's or Rose Hill | F. King's Cove |

[1] On Good Friday, 1929, Mrs. Bolton, Mrs. Hodgdon, Miss Gregory
and I stood on Great Hill. The day was clear and cold. To the north
lay Peddock's Island, Hull, and Point Allerton, all dotted with cottages.
To the west lay the low lands of "Germantown" and the higher ground
of Hough's Neck, sparsely inhabited. To the south lay Rowe's Hill, with
Hunt's Hill beyond, mere rises, covered by small cottages. Beyond them
was the home of the King Cove Boat Club on Hunt's Hill Point, from
which King's Cove made an inward arc to the bridge.

Wessagusset (wearing bank), the Indian name of the site, was the first permanent or continuous settlement to be made within the original colony of the Massachusetts Bay.

Into the forest stillness came Weston's men. Captain John Smith's book had promised herring and cod, salmon and mullets, as well as salt, timber, pitch; and in the animal world beavers, otters, martens and foxes. Smith was no alchemist and could not promise beyond what he knew, but he was sure that there were base metals in the country and he hinted at gold and silver. Corn and berries he could vouch for. Hawks, cranes and ducks he no doubt had seen, as well as cunners and crabs, lobsters, oysters and clams.

Weston's larger company — some 60 men — arrived in August, 1622, and proceeded to make Wessagusset, near the present Weymouth, their home. The summer was too far gone for planting. The men were wasteful and soon came to famine. They were, said Weston, "*rude* [uneducated?] fellows" from the London streets. The Indians were watchful and asked, "Why do your men and dogs die?" They began to tell tales of shipwrecked Frenchmen whom they had enslaved and tortured. The English bartered their coats and blankets for corn and did menial work for the red men to obtain food. They stole from the savages, and at last were forced to placate them by hanging publicly a thief.

Pratt heard that the sachems planned to destroy both Wessagusset and Plymouth. He set forth about

WESSAGUSSET FROM GREAT HILL

The site is one-half inch above the top of the tree nearest the bottom of the picture

46

the 23d of March, 1622–23, with snow still on the ground, to warn Governor Bradford at Plymouth. He ran on till the sun went down red in the west and Ursa Major and the pole star came out. He crossed a cold river, listened to the howling of wolves, and at last in a deep dell made a fire. He was lost and his pursuers therefore missed him. The next afternoon Pratt hailed John Hampden with the words: "Mr. Hamdin, I am glad to see you alive!" He then reached Plymouth and gave the alarm.

Standish was sent by Bradford with eight men and an Indian guide to investigate the situation at Wessagusset. He found the men scattered and unarmed, ready to become an easy prey. While he discussed with them the problem of food supply and defence, menacing messages and threats came from two sachems, Pecksuot and Wituwaumet. Standish with three soldiers got the chiefs into a room with two other Indians. The door was shut and he stabbed Pecksuot. The other Indians thus trapped fought silently and courageously until Wituwaumet also was killed. Five more Indians were soon done to death.

The Indian conspiracy had its justification in the conduct of Weston's men who, when starvation stared them in the face, cheated and robbed the Indians and abused their women. Bradford thinks that the retaliatory slaughter was necessary, or, in other words, that the end (their safety) justified treachery and murder. The incident grieved the friends of the Pilgrims who remained in Holland, but Mr. Adams is inclined to

take the Bradford view — that the Indians "by the
good providence of god were taken in their owne
snare, and ther wickednes came upon their owne
pate." After this bloody fight Weston's "pale and
houses" were abandoned, and remained unused until
Gorges and his company arrived in the autumn, prepared to set up Episcopacy in New England. Some
of the Weston survivors went home; others to Virginia and to Plymouth. Nine of the "60 lusty men"
had died of famine, two were slain by Indians, one
died on a fishing ship, and four were reported to be
with Levett at Casco Bay.

It will be seen that Weston's poorly prepared colony existed only until April, 1623. The settlers had
fled and two or three stragglers whom they left behind had been put to death. Through the succeeding summer the blockhouse stood unoccupied. But
in September of the same year Captain Robert Gorges
landed at Wessagusset, having a grant of land and
authority to set up a government worthy of the name.
He was to be a "Lieutenant General" with powers
ecclesiastical, civil and criminal. The Council for
New England had grandiose designs and the Gorges
colony included able men as well as women and children. Among these were several who were to be
heard from later. The Rev. William Morrell came
with authority which foreshadowed Episcopacy; the
Rev. William Blaxton was a scholar; Samuel Maverick and William Jeffreys were gentlemen of wealth
and culture. Thomas Walford, a blacksmith, John

Bursley or Burslem, and several others whose names appear in the meagre records of the period must also have come with Gorges.

The Boston Harbor enterprises were unfortunate in their leaders. Gorges, it appears, had learned little or nothing of Smith's gospel of codfish and work, which gospel did not in his opinion suit a gentleman of his "quallitie & condition." He went home in disgust in the spring of 1624, taking some of his company with him, while others sought the more moderate climate of Virginia. A few remained, with Morrell as their leader, and were helped with supplies from Plymouth. Morrell was a man of gentle temperament; he did not assert his ecclesiastical authority, which would have antagonized the Plymouth settlers, but spent his leisure in composing a creditable poem on his new home at Wessagusset. He wrote:

> O happie planter, if you knew the height
> Of planters honours where ther's such delight;
> There Nature's bounties though not planted are,
> Great store and sorts of berries great and faire:
> The Filberd, Cherry, and the fruitful Vine,
> Which cheares the heart and makes it more divine.
> Earth's spangled beauties pleasing smell and sight;
> Objects for gallant choyce and chiefe delight.
> A ground-Nut there runnes on a grassie threed,
> Along the shallow earth as in a bed,
> Yealow without, thin filmd, sweete, lilly white,
> Of strength to feede and cheare the appetite.

Governor Bradford of Plymouth records the departure of Morrell for England in the spring of 1625.

MAP OF CAPE ANN HARBOR

Some of the party lingered on at Wessagusset and gave the settlement later known as Weymouth a continuous history. With them Thomas Morton of Merrymount, two miles away, used to pass long winter evenings. But the loss of a man of Morrell's refinement and learning was a distinct misfortune to which may perhaps be attributed the desire of some of the settlers to establish new homes in other parts of the Bay.

The Rev. John Lyford reached Plymouth in the spring of 1624, and became intimate with John Oldham who had come the year before. Together they tried to institute Episcopal ceremonies and Lyford, it is said, baptized a child of William Hilton who had not joined the Plymouth congregation. In so doing Lyford undoubtedly represented the convictions of a faction among the merchant adventurers, but he and Oldham were opposing the Governor. Both were banished from the colony in 1624. Hubbard never saw the humor of his characterization of these two able men, Lyford and Oldham: "Some of their friends," he writes, "do affirm that both were looked upon as seemingly at least religious." They moved to Natascot where they were joined by Roger Conant, called by his neighbor Hubbard, the historian, "a pious, sober and prudent gentleman." The group soon had a following. Conant the next year was appointed through the influence of the Rev. John White of the Dorchester company governor of the new settlement at Cape Ann (on the west side of

Gloucester harbor), and took with him late in 1625 Lyford, Thomas Gray, Walter Knight and some others.

The ship *Charity* had brought 14 settlers to Cape Ann in 1624. Humphrey Woodbury in 1680 testified: "My father John Woodberye did about 56 yeares agoe remooue for new England, & I then traveled with him as farr as Dorchester, and I vnderstood that my father came to New England by order of a company caled Dorchester Company, & that my father & the company with him brought cattle & other things to Cape Ann for plantation work, & built an house & keept theire cattell & sett up fishing." J. J. Babson in 1854 wrote that "Fisherman's field" was the spot occupied by the English at Cape Ann in 1624. It contained 100 acres and commenced at the westerly end of the beach, on the north side of the harbor. On its westerly side it was skirted by the road to Manchester which separates it from a range of hills. On the seaward side it had two coves, one very small, formed by a rocky bluff called Stage Head. The arable land, said Christopher Levett in 1624, was too limited and the fishing fields too far away for good success.

John Oldham was offered the position of overseer of trade at Cape Ann but preferred to remain at Natascot. In 1626 he set out for Virginia but nearly lost his life on the Cape Cod shoals. He became reconciled to the people about him and, moving to Watertown, represented the town in the first General

Court. He bought Prudence Island and from there carried on trade with the Narragansett Indians. In July, 1636, John Gallop of Boston encountered Oldham's pinnace off Block Island, her deck occupied by 14 Indians. With his crew of two young sons and a hired man Gallop opened fire and rammed the pinnace. After a sanguinary fight he boarded the pinnace while his crew covered him with their guns. In the stern sheets he saw a corpse under a seine. It was still warm; the skull was cleft and the hands and feet were in process of being amputated. Gallop washed the blood from the dead man's face and exclaimed:

"Ah! Brother Oldham, is it thou? I am resolved to avenge thy blood!"

JOHN OLDHAM

The body was buried in the sea. Thus ended the career of an able man, sometimes called a "thorn" of the Pilgrim fathers.[1]

An incident of the summer of 1624 was destined to make both litigation and literature. Captain Wollaston of the *Unity*, "a man of pretie parts," as Bradford calls him, and Humphrey Rastell, a London merchant engaged in transporting indentured servants to Virginia, but now supercargo on Weston's ship the *Swan*, set out from Blackwall, London, in the

[1] Goodwin's Pilgrim Republic, page 273.

early summer on a voyage to Virginia. There was
discord from the start. Captain John Martin was
to be taken over with twelve servants, for all of whom
he paid. Five of them with tickets were not allowed
aboard and the ships sailed without them. Head
winds and a leak, as well as the wish to meet with a
certain ship in New England, led the two leaders to
change their course. They put in at Cape Ann and
no doubt visited Wessagusset. Hereabouts they remained for nine weeks, Martin fretting to be off.
Among the party were William Holland, gentleman,
who seems to have been mild enough, Thomas Morton, later to make trouble, and Lieutenant Fitcher.
Food ran low and the men had but a biscuit a day,
bad meat twice a week, very little butter, oatmeal or
beer.

Martin, a man of importance, asked how long he
was to be kept a prisoner, and Mr. Rastell, grown
"collericke and hott," said that not the King nor the
Lords of the Council of England would stir him
until he thought good to go. Martin said that the
leaders waited for a chance to kill him.

Finally Captain Wollaston set off for Virginia,
leaving part of the company to form a camp
near Wessagusset and await his orders. Later he
directed Rastell to follow him to Virginia, leaving Lieutenant Fitcher behind in command of the
dozen men at the camp which they called Mt.
Wollaston. Morton, one of these, soon led a rebel-
lion and turned Fitcher "out of doors." He then re-

VIEW OF MT. WOLLASTON

named the camp Merrymount and began a reign of *laissez-faire* from which he has been dubbed "the Lord of Misrule." The decision of the Court on Martin's case was delivered in November, 1624, and went against Rastell.

Mt. Wollaston was a rounded hillock surmounted by a red cedar which lived on until 1850. Charles Francis Adams saw the dead trunk in 1882.[1]

At this period New England appeared to the European as a beautiful, irregular coast of deep bays, great rivers, rocky headlands and wooded islands. Here and there an intervale or river meadow could be seen, but for the most part forests were everywhere. The first fishermen and trappers chose for their camps islands near the mainland with good harbors, such as Damariscove and Richmond Island, and peninsulas like Cape Ann which had advantages in traffic with the natives. At one of these points the adventurers would erect a long plain barn, with a fireplace at one end where cranes for large pots and spits for broiling were placed. Along the walls were bunks for the "servants." The rest of the great barn was for storing barrels of salt, skins, dried fish and fish in hogsheads of brine. The atmosphere must have been freighted with a variety of odors.

Near this great warehouse were perhaps two or three cabins for the officials, and a large platform or stage on which the fish were split, salted and dried. If on the mainland, a palisade or a ditch may have

[1] It blew down in 1898, was removed in 1919, and Mrs. Ronald Dummer reports seeing the trunk in 1929.

been constructed as a protection from a surprise attack. Not far away were usually a few wigwams of Indians attracted to the fishermen by hope of barter in knives, beads, cloth, and strong drink. They knew that beaver skins and corn were wanted by white men at every trading post.

The life offered at such a camp was rough and hazardous. Good men were to be found there, but many of the leaders and servants were hard drinkers and not too scrupulous. Bagnall at Richmond Island and Oldham of the Rhode Island trade paid with their lives the price of sharp dealing. The only diversion was afforded by the arrival of ships from England, France, New Amsterdam and Virginia. Old friendships were renewed, old quarrels reopened. We can hear the angry words at Damerill's Cove when one Cornish came on board ship to ask why his brother had been executed; or the fierce debate between Humphrey Rastell and his passenger, John Martin, in Cape Ann harbor where Rastell idled or was delayed from week to week before going on to Virginia.

Between work, drinking, and fighting, the trading post life along the New England coast from 1615 to 1640 offered little to attract wives or clergymen, but it appealed to men of courage in an age of adventure.

Various happenings at Cape Ann came to the ears of Governor Bradford at Plymouth and his advisers. Title to this land was claimed by the Plymouth colony, and the planters were again ousted. They then

# NEW ENGLISH CANAAN
## OR
# NEW CANAAN.

## Containing an Abstract of New England,

*Composed in three Bookes.*

The first Booke setting forth the originall of the Natives, their
Manners and Customes, together with their tractable Nature and
Love towards the English.

The second Booke setting forth the naturall Indowments of the
Country, and what staple Commodities it
yealdeth.

The third Booke setting forth, what people are planted there,
their prosperity, what remarkable accidents have happened since the first
planting of it, together with their Tenents and practise
of their Church.

*Written by* Thomas Morton of Cliffords Inne gent, *upon tenne
yeares knowledge and experiment of the
Country.*

Printed at AMSTERDAM,
*By* JACOB FREDERICK STAM.
*In the Yeare* 1637.

moved late in 1626 to Naumkeag (Salem). Here Church of England services were maintained until 1628.

The Cape Ann charter fell into the hands of a group of men headed by Matthew Cradock. When their agent, John Endecott, appeared, 6 September, 1628, Conant lost his authority. Two of Endecott's chief supporters, John and Samuel Brown, went over to Conant's party and were banished a few weeks later. Conant, however, gave up the fight for his own form of worship and lived in peace till his death in 1679. Early writers called him "a most religious, prudent and worthy gentleman."

In the autumn of 1628 the most prosperous plantations in New England were Plymouth, Wessagusset and Piscataqua, ranking above Salem, Natascot, Shawmut and Hilton's Point (Dover). Two years later (September, 1630) Shawmut (now Boston), Watertown, Charlestown, Dorchester and Roxbury led in sums levied on the Bay colony towns. The other settlements mentioned above were outside the jurisdiction.

ST. MARY'S CHURCH, HORNCASTLE
Where Rev. William Blaxton was baptized

## IV

## MR. BLAXTON COMES TO SHAWMUT

TO American travelers Lincolnshire recalls
the Cathedral, one of the most beautiful in
England. To Bostonians the old town on
the Witham with its very tall spire is another asso-
ciation with the county. At Norwich Robert Browne
organized a congregation of those who believed with
him that each church should be "a law unto itself,"
and through his followers brought about the migration of the Pilgrim Fathers to the New World. But
there are many other ties with this land of level
meadows, hayricks and lean-to farmhouses.

At Willoughby by Alford, a village south of Louth
in the same county, Captain John Smith, that famous
adventurer over the known world, and narrator of
unbelievable tales, was born in the winter of 1579/80.
It is reasonable to assume that his books were talked
about in vicarages and manor houses of the neighborhood, if indeed he did not return occasionally to keep
his memory green by contact with his boyhood companions. Thus it is possible that John and Agnes
(Hawley) Blaxton, who lived at Horncastle, a few
miles away, discussed exploration in their family
circle as any parents might be expected to do. Two
children, Frances and John, had already been born
when William, the future inhabitant of Shawmut,

now Boston, came into the Blaxton home. He was christened at St. Mary's, the parish church of Horncastle, 5 March, 1595/96. The next year a daughter Ann was born; then Merial, who was named for her grandmother, Merial Clark, wife of Richard Blaxton, came two and a half years later (1599). Finally on 12 December, 1600, George was born. Just six years had been given to William to know his mother — the impressionable years — when we read this entry in the parish register:

"Agnes, whose death many lamented, wife of John Blaxton, buried 8 Dec. 1602."

From the simple tribute recorded above (the first and almost the only mention of personal virtues in the dull book of life and death entries at Horncastle) much may be pictured of the Blaxton home. John, the older brother of William, entered Emmanuel College, Cambridge, in 1610, living at his own expense. He received his Bachelor's degree in 1613/14 and his Master's degree in 1617, being ordained to the ministry at Peterboro the same year. He may be the Rev. John Blaxton, a "painful minister" at Osmington, Dorset, for at least 28 years, and a vigorous pamphleteer who condemned the rapacity and idleness of the clergy of his day. He was there in 1642.

William, if we may judge from what we know of his later career, was a quiet, studious boy, too fond perhaps of solitude. He probably attended King Edward's Grammar School at Horncastle which had been revived in 1571 by a grant issued to the Earl of

Lincoln. Horncastle was not unlike other towns of its size. It had its maypole, its pit where cocks waged their bloody battles, and its ring and rope for the cruel sport of bull baiting. But if we read aright his character and the influence of his home he saw nothing of these rough and brutal pastimes.

In the spring of 1610 both of William's grandparents died, and in July his oldest sister married. He was admitted a "sizar" of Emmanuel College in 1614, being assisted by an allowance from the college, and received his degree in the winter of 1617/18. William was ordained at Peterboro in 1619, but did not receive his Master's degree until 1621. Blaxton was now ready to take up the work for which he had prepared himself. The late Mr. Thomas C. Amory (Bostonian Soc. Coll., vol. 1, no. 1) in his delightful sketch of Blaxton concedes that he came over with Robert Gorges in 1623, but states that the young clergyman was "a non-conformist and detested prelacy, as exhibited in Bancroft and Laud. His canonical coat, which Johnson tells us he continued to wear in America, shows that he was still attached to the English Church, and regarded himself as a teacher of its tenets."

FERDINANDO GORGES

Blaxton's liking for non-conformity seems to me to be unfounded conjecture. Mr. Adams in his "Old Planters" shows that Sir Ferdinando Gorges had in mind "his favorite scheme of establishing Episcopacy in New England" when he sent his son to Wessagusset with Mr. Morrell, "a sort of vicarious primate" who was to exercise superintendence over churches established in the colony. With him went Mr. Samuel Maverick, a layman who later wrote bitterly of non-conformist bigotry; William Jeffreys, who continued on at Wessagusset and eventually got into trouble because the dissenters did not like the Church of England atmosphere of the services there; Thomas Walford, who was banished from his home on the south side of Breed's Hill and became a church warden in Portsmouth; and Rev. William Blaxton who, after five years of Puritan rule in Boston, sold his property and migrated to Rhode Island.

Blaxton, we have every reason to believe, loved the Church of England. He could have had no very great sympathy for the non-conformist teaching at Emmanuel College or he would not have set sail with Gorges in 1623. It was, however, a favorable time in his personal affairs for a voyage to America. His father had just died, and there were no home responsibilities that could not easily be borne by other members of the family.

When the Gorges company went on shore at the cove by the little hill at Wessagusset they found a "pale" (perhaps a palisade), and a blockhouse or

# A
# VOYAGE
# INTO NEVV
# ENGLAND

Begun in 1 6 2 3. and ended
in 1 6 2 4.

Performed by CHRISTOPHER LEVETT,
his Maiesties Woodward of *Somerset shire*, and
one of the Councell of New-England.

Yorkes                                             Bonauen:
ture.

C. 2470

Printed at LONDON, by WILLIAM IONES,
and are to be sold by *Edward Brewster*, at the signe
of the Bible in Paules Church yard,
1628.

ruined dwelling with, no doubt, blackened stones
where hearths had been.  Blaxton and Morrell must
have spent the autumn in doing their part toward
constructing houses, as well as in study and preach-
ing.  Possibly they journeyed to Plymouth, 44 miles
away.

The winter of 1623–24 was a snowy one, says
Christopher Levett, a shipmaster who built a fortified shelter on "House Island" in Casco Bay, near
Portland.  So we may imagine the Gorges colony
more or less "snowed in" until the spring of 1624.

We know that Gorges seized a vessel owned by
Thomas Weston and explored the coast as far as
"Little Harbor," at the mouth of the Piscataqua
River.  There he conversed with David Thomson, a
Scotch merchant from Plymouth, England, who had
but recently arrived with a grant in his pocket.  He
also met Christopher Levett, who was exploring for
a settlement.

It does not require great imagination to picture the
conversations which three such men as Levett, Thomson and Robert Gorges held at Little Harbor at their
first meeting.  Thomson was the shrewd man of business, familiar with all the enterprises for colonizing
New England through his former position in England as agent for the Council.  Gorges had but recently brought over a company to settle in Wessagusset where Weston had made a failure a few
months before.  Levett was full of enthusiasm for the
Maine coast, and was about to make a feeble and alto-

gether hopeless settlement in Casco Bay that he might honor the old city of York. Each had his story to tell; one of much accomplished, another of feeble beginnings, and a third of hopes not yet come to fruition. The climate, the Indians, and the fishing must have filled many an hour of ardent discussion.

There were, however, lighter moments when, as the three men sat before the fire with glass and pipe, stories characteristic of such colonizing days were recounted with gusto. It was Robert Gorges, I think,[1] who told the story of a man named Chapman, a Londoner, who enacted with his two servants an adventure similar to the now famous story of the Admirable Crichton. When the Gorges ship, the *Katharine,* arrived at Plymouth, she lay at anchor for some time in the harbor. Chapman, who had brought with him enough provisions for eighteen months for himself and his two servants, went ashore. There in that model hamlet of good people he managed to dispose of his entire store of provisions in less than five months, spending each week one-tenth of his whole hoardings on wine, tobacco, and immoral women. As an illustration, the narrator instanced an exchange of a suit of clothes for tobacco having only one-twentieth the value of the clothing. At last Chapman became a servant to his servant. The new master, however, had no such weakness of character. He offered Chap-

---

[1] Christopher Levett of York (Baxter), page 126. On page 125 Levett refers to Weston's 1622 colony as "about two yeares since." Therefore his next reference to "this last yeare there went over diverse at one time" would seem to indicate the 1623 settlement of Gorges. Since Gorges himself met Levett at Little Harbor in 1624, the story may well have come from him.

man "one bisket cake" a day if he would work, and one-half a cake for each day of idleness. Chapman, true to his character, chose the half cake. In five months from his arrival he was dead.

This story may be said to throw light on life in Plymouth as well as upon a certain type of colonist with whom managers of trading companies had to deal.[1]

The far more serious purpose of the meeting at Little Harbor was to organize a government for New England, composed of Captain Robert Gorges, lieutenant general; Captain Francis West, admiral; Christopher Levett, David Thomson, and two men from New Plymouth, councillors. The Rev. William Morrell was commanded to superintend the establishment of the Church of England form of worship throughout the territory. Those of this group who were present took the oath.[2]

*[signature]*

CHRISTOPHER LEVETT

The return of Gorges to Wessagusset must have created many new topics for discussion.

At this time, it will be remembered, settlements were very few, those at Monhegan Island and Damariscove Island on the Maine coast, Piscataqua, Plymouth, and a few other places. So said Bradford. No doubt the feeling of isolation was more than some could endure. Gorges in the spring of

---

[1] Bradford sent back to England several unfit immigrants who had come in the *Anne* and *Little James* in July, 1623.

[2] A. Brown's First Republic in America, 1898, page 566.

1624 went to Plymouth and took ship for England. Many of the company accompanied him, and the depression caused by such desertions must have fallen heavily on Morrell, Jeffreys, and Blaxton, leaders of those who remained.

We know so little about Mr. Blaxton's life that any fact is worthy of record. Mr. Adams has called attention to Governor Winthrop's note dated 10 February, 1631, that "it hath been observed ever since this bay was planted by Englishmen, viz., seven years, that at this day the frost hath broken up every year." Thus from 1624 on some one had kept a weather diary, and Mr. Blaxton's manuscripts destroyed in King Philip's War would seem to have contained these local records.

From Plymouth and perhaps from Natascot (Hull) may have come items of news during that barren winter of 1624–25. At Plymouth the chief event of the winter of 1624–25, if Bradford's History is an indication, is the quarrel with Lyford and Oldham. These men chafed under the Separatist rule and wrote letters home by Captain Peirce's ship.[1] After she had sailed "the Govᵣ and some other of his freinds tooke a shalop and wente out with the ship a league or 2, to sea, and caled for all Lifords and Oldums letters." Bradford found above twenty, many large and "full of slanders and false accusations." From these letters he learned that they planned "a reformation in church and commone-

---

[1] Robert Hicks and many others were supposed to be hostile to Bradford and friendly to the aims of the Adventurers in England.

wealth," and that they "intended to joyne togeather and have the sacrements."

Governor Bradford kept secret the fact that he had read the letters and had made copies of some of them. He watched the two opposition leaders until he thought it wise to arrest them. The whole incident filled the winter months in Plymouth with bitterness and excitement. The story in all varieties of form must have been the talk of the colony. It was a forerunner of many banishments to come on account of a determination to stifle free worship in the colony of New Plymouth. Perhaps the explanation of this policy is to be found in Dr. Morison's assertion that the Governor "regarded the colony as an overseas Congregational church and conducted it as such whenever possible."[1]

Bradford was in a difficult position, a young man of thirty-four at the head of a minority party in Plymouth, with the managing merchants in London out of sympathy with his views. Lyford called the separatists "the smalest number in the collony." Banks says: "It can be established beyond a reasonable doubt that these separatists were in the minority from the first landing in Plymouth." It was Bradford's salvation, however, that the small group of freemen gave their governor "almost complete discretionary authority"; and he said that he allowed the generality a share in the government "only in some weighty maters when we thinke good."

[1] Dict. of American Biography, volume 2. Dr. Morison's excellent sketch.

ENTRANCE TO THE PISCATAQUA

The Rev. John Robinson, having been refused passage to New England, the people had been without a clergyman for four years — perhaps the only colony so bereft. Then Lyford was sent out by vote of the London officials to administer to the majority if not to all the colonists. He was then a man of about forty-eight years of age.

We can only guess at the names of those who "with tears" appealed to Lyford to perform the rites of baptism, marriage and burial. Oldham and the nine who came with him at their own expense formed a strong group. Others may have come in the same manner, and left no record. In any case the "particulars," as they were called, were among the discontented, and some seem to have been sent back by the Governor. John Billington on the other hand was not a "particular," but he and his circle supported Lyford.[1] Hilton's family from Cheshire were of course with him, having had their child baptized. Others from Cheshire may have joined them, including Francis Sprague, the turbulent innkeeper, and Robert Ratliffe, who left Plymouth some years later. The Southwark group were probably discontented, and Robert Hicks was one of these. His son-in-law, Edward Bangs, and Clement Briggs, who had lived with Hicks in Southwark, can be added. Edward Burcher was another, and he soon moved out of Plymouth. Thomas Flavel's family from Southwark soon left the colony. Since Christopher Conant

---

[1] Billington was the leader of a group. Morton refers to him as "beloved of many."

did not abide long he probably was (like his brother Roger) dissatisfied with public policies. Anthony Dix, either through discontent or for convenience as a mariner, moved northward. It is not strange that Bradford wrote in alarm to his father-in-law that the situation was grave. These happenings were indeed sure to interest Morrell and Blaxton of the Established Church as they walked together on the little beach at Wessagusset.

When the ship *Discovery,* with John Pory, Secretary of Virginia, on board, dropped into Plymouth harbor in the autumn of 1622, the Secretary met his friend Governor Bradford. Later Pory, in a letter, described the town. It had a substantial palisade of 2,700 feet in circumference, stronger than any in Virginia, with a blockhouse on a mount, commanding all the harbor.[1] He adds that the people were relatively free from vice and wickedness.

Captain John Smith at this time was interviewing travelers, and writing to the colonists, such as William Hilton of Piscataqua, for information. He published the result of his labors in 1624 under the title "Advertisements for Unexperienced Planters." He confirms Pory's observations and adds some details. There were 25 houses, seven more having been burnt. The Fort, built of stone, wood, and earthworks, had a watch tower, and ordnance well mounted.

At Hull, known as Natascot, a fishing village about seven miles from Shawmut by sea and twenty by

[1] The present city of Cambridge had a palisade in 1632.

VIEW OF NATASCOT (HULL)

land, a few families subsisted at this time. Their names are variously given as Thomas and John Gray, and Walter Knight. Others, like John Oldham, Rev. John Lyford, and Roger Conant, did not come till later. Half a dozen men still clung to Mt. Wollaston with Thomas Morton.

If there was little intercourse between Blaxton's friends at Wessagusset and these men at Natascot, or with David Thomson and the Hiltons at Piscataqua, there were connections with Plymouth from which Mr. Morrell was already planning to depart in the spring for England. This momentous event must have engaged Mr. Blaxton's thought during the entire winter, for he had no desire to return to England, and the nearest settlement at Plymouth would not be congenial. Indeed other plans were in the making. Samuel Maverick, Thomas Walford, and possibly Mr. Thomson, were already contemplating with him a removal to new homes in the Bay, and each one was to choose a site which would in time be known as a centre of population.

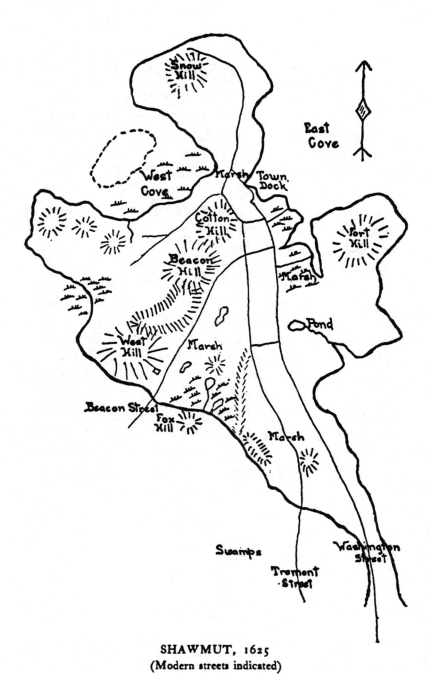

Snow
Hill

East
Cove

West
Cove

Marsh Town
Dock

Cotton
Hill

Fort
Hill

Beacon
Hill

Marsh

Pond

West
Hill

Marsh

Beacon Street

Fox
Hill

Marsh

Swamps

Washington
Street

Tremont
Street

SHAWMUT, 1625
(Modern streets indicated)

# SHAWMUT IN MR. BLAXTON'S DAY

AS the ice age passed into unrecorded history it left behind a great plain which has been called the Boston basin. Here and there were drumlins, hills of varying size composed of gravel and sand, deposited by the ice. Whether of the same composition or not, they must have had the appearance of the sugar-loaf hills that are a marked feature of the southern slopes of the Penine Range in Westmorland and Yorkshire. When our Boston basin settled to a point where the sea surged in over the land, some of these hills disappeared from view; others reared their tops above the Bay as islands. Most conspicuous of these were the three hills between the Charles River and the harbor, known now as Snow Hill[1] to the north, Beacon Hill to the west, and Fort Hill to the east, connected by marsh land, and with fields covered by berry bushes, rose bushes, alder, and a few trees. Gradually the sandy flats between this group of hills and the present Roxbury mainland grew into a slender ridge, making a peninsula which was called by the Indians, Shawmut.

Snow Hill, the eminence west of the Old North Church, rose to about 50 feet, with a cliff-like steepness to the north. A spur jutted out into the river at the west, sometimes known as Hudson's Point, named

[1] Windmill Hill or Copp's Hill.

after an early ferryman. The peak of the hill was near the junction of Snow Hill Street with Hull Street.

At the east was Fort Hill, rising to about 80 feet, a conspicuous object to mariners coming into the harbor. It could easily be fortified, since it was surrounded on three sides by water and marsh, approach by land being had from the south over what is now High Street and across Congress Street. The northern side of the hill was a bluff.

The great hill of Shawmut, however, was the range which ran from east to west across the peninsula beginning at Dock Square (in front of the Faneuil Hall Market) and extending westward to Charles Street (by the colored people's church). Although it had three peaks, it looks in early pictures not unlike Penhill Beacon, the splendid high ridge on which Mary Queen of Scots looked from her chamber prison at Bolton Castle. It dominated the scene and with its slopes absorbed the heart of present day Boston. With this hill the Rev. William Blaxton, the first settler, will forever be associated.

*William Blaxton*

WILLIAM BLAXTON

At the eastern end of the ridge the crown was called Cotton Hill, with its peak at the southerly end of Pemberton Square. From the easterly slope of Cotton Hill several springs sent streams from the gravelly soil down the bank to a cove whose site is known

EAST SHORE OF BOSTON, 1625, FROM FORT HILL

Atlantic Avenue now runs from the lower right corner to the point just above the tree

as Dock Square. This land, Pemberton Square and Cornhill, was usually very wet, and attracted voyagers in search of fresh water for their casks. It is not too rash to assert that the crews of French fishing vessels had anchored off this cove in the fishing season, during the 50 or 75 years before Mr. Blaxton came here in 1625 from Wessagusset down the Bay. Indeed some chroniclers, more venturesome than I, assert that as many as 200 ships from France came to the Grand Banks in a single year to catch cod. "Some of them," as Gosnold states, "fell down the coast for corn and water as well as to engage in barter with the red men." In 1602 he found savages dressed in "Christian" clothing which they had obtained from fishermen. Dock Square was for at least a century the landing place for these transient mariners.

Between Cotton Hill and its westerly neighbor, Beacon Hill, the slope to the north ended in a marsh (Valley acre). Out of it (at Howard Street) flowed a rivulet along Sudbury Street to the edge of the great western cove at Haymarket Square. Beacon Hill, itself, rose to 150 feet above mean low tide, its peak being about where Ashburton Place joins Bowdoin Street. Its gaunt outline was an awesome sight against the night sky. There are fleeting proofs that from its southwesterly slope (Hancock Place) a spring sent a stream down the hillside through the tip of the Common and along Winter Street, bearing then to the south until it reached the well-known pond between Avon and Bedford Streets. From this pond

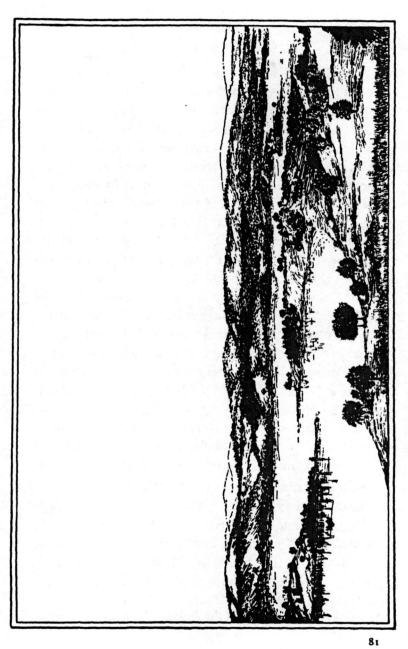

THE NORTH END OF BOSTON, 1625, FROM WEST HILL

our Beacon Hill waters took the course of Bedford Street to the sea marsh at the head of Kingston Street.

West of Joy Street the ridge rose again to a peak just east of Louisburg Square, called "West Hill" or "Mount Whoredom." Hereabouts I suppose Captain Byron stood in 1764 when he made two of the water-color drawings of old Boston, now in the rooms of the Bostonian Society. He saw the city before any marked change in the coast line had been made. On the west slope water gushed from the ground at the present north end of the Square, and trickled down into a pond or marsh which occupied part of the site of West Cedar Street, only a few feet east of the old shore line. Mr. Chamberlain tells me that there were other springs on the westerly slope of "West Hill."

The spring at the southwestern corner of Chestnut and Spruce Streets (a neighbor of the spring in Louisburg Square) may have led the Rev. William Blaxton to settle on this spot. Here he lived for some ten years, keeping his vegetables and his roses, his pigs and possibly a cow, reading his favorite books, and noting the weather with great exactitude.

South of Mr. Blaxton's house was a stretch of desolate marsh and sand — at least, so it appears in Captain Byron's sketch, — relieved by two or three little hummocks, and reaching southerly to a ridge, now the path from the head of West Street to Park Square. The western bound of this marsh or common was the swampy line of water which ran in a concave arc just east of Charles Street; and a drum-

THE SOUTH END OF BOSTON, 1625, FROM WEST HILL

Fox Hill and Common in the foreground ; Back Bay on the right ; The Neck (Washington Street) beyond

lin, called Fox Hill, raised its sandy head at a point now just inside the southeasterly corner of the Public Garden. The space between West Hill (Mr. Blaxton's house) and the ridge walk was divided by a hill where the Civil War monument and German gun now stand, with its western slope still a favorite toboggan slide for boys in winter. On either side was a marshy pool, the northerly one now being known as the Frog Pond.

There were few trees in Shawmut, but along the beachy and swampy neck of land to the south — the narrowest part between Castle and Dover Streets — there were trees for many years. Some were cut for fuel by early settlers until the town fathers put a stop to it. Here and there on the Beacon Hill ridge were a few elms and cedars, but most of the soil was covered with scrub and wild flowers.

As late as the boyhood days of Mr. Michael J. Canavan, a student of Boston topography, the marshes of the Columbus Avenue district still remained. Mr. Russell Gray has told me that as a boy he used to swim across the Charles River to a swimming pool not so very far from the home of the President of the Massachusetts Institute of Technology. So it is that the Boston of Mr. Blaxton's day has been altered even so late as in our own generation by the filling in of cove, marsh and pond, the lowering of hills, the leading of rivulets through culverts, and the enlargement of Boston's bounds by pushing away from the three hills the coast line which Nature made.

# VI

## MR. BLAXTON'S LIFE AND TIMES

THE year 1625 opened with great local events in store for it, as far as Wessagusset was to be concerned. The sequence of these happenings cannot be surely fixed because Mr. Blaxton's ten manuscript volumes which he left behind him at his death on "Study Hill" were burned in King Philip's War.

When the return of Mr. Morrell to England became a fact, Mr. Blaxton no doubt prepared to move his library and his manuscripts to Shawmut. Such a step required not only planning but exploration. He must have tramped the shore line of Shawmut either during the autumn of 1624 or early in the spring of 1625. As it was then the custom to travel by water, he would cross over to the peninsula by boat. No doubt Mr. Maverick and possibly Walford and others took part in these adventures. Myles Standish at Plymouth and men at Wessagusset could offer advice to aid him.

We can imagine Blaxton's farewell to the Rev. Mr. Morrell, and his own departure from Wessagusset in a heavily laden boat soon after. Passing out through Weymouth Fore River, as we call it, he would skirt the shore of Mt. Wollaston until he came to Squantum; thence with a large island (later

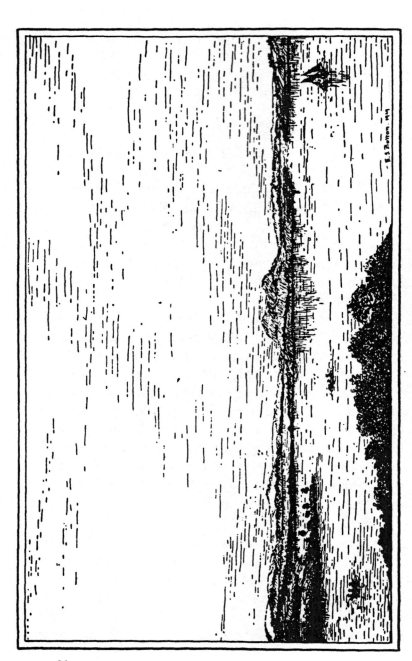

BOSTON FROM DORCHESTER NECK

settled by David Thomson) on his right he would
head for Castle Island and Conant's or Governor's
Island.  Turning west he would cross two miles of
open water and make for the sandy cove now known
as Dock Square, on the eastern side of the peninsula
and at the foot of a great hill.  Maverick, some years
later, wrote of this Shawmut, now Boston, as "lying
pleasantly on a plaine and the ascending of a High
Mount which lyes about the midle of ye plaine."

Blaxton and his helpers carried his goods up the
wet hill-slope, now known as Cornhill, over the path
already made by himself along the line of the present Tremont Street and Beacon Street, to the western
side of the peninsula, thus skirting the lower and
southern edge of the "High Mount" all the way.
What a momentous journey his destiny made it!  At
the end of the path and by the shore of the Charles'
River marshes he prepared to build his shelter.  It
can be located presumably just west of Spruce Street,
an area well watered with numerous springs.  Some
still break forth at long intervals in spite of walls and
pavements.

Below his home site were sandy marsh lands from
which rose a drumlin later known as Fox Hill.  The
very view which met his eyes has been preserved for
us in the water-color sketch by Captain Byron of the
British navy.

I have often wondered what manner of cottage
Blaxton built for himself.  As a college man of good
family, bred to life in an English manor house, and

having a library to be protected, he would want more than a shack. Stones for the foundation were to be had close to his hand, but timber nearer than the "Neck" could not have been plentiful.

It would seem to me probable that the young clergyman (he was just thirty), if he did not at first live under cloth, would lay a foundation of loose stones and construct a rough, one room shelter of logs. Whether these logs were squared with an adze or not we can only surmise. No early record of such a house has come down to us. Wigwams made of boughs[1] were too inflammable for a man fond of his books. Huts were built of vertical logs, either with sharpened ends driven into the earth or with the ends set in a trench. The tops were held in line and roofed over, the rain being kept out by thatch, which, said Edward Wynne of Newfoundland in 1622, when made of sedge, flags, and rushes, was better than boards both for warmth and for tightness.[2] The houses at Cape Ann in 1623 were thatched. Andrew Davis wrote that, lacking lime, the chimney was made of "small strips of wood laid at right angles to each other, one on top of another and locked together at the corners by gravity, the cracks between the strips being filled with mud and the inside surface of the chimney covered with a coating of clay."[3]

---

[1] Levett, at Saco, in 1623, built a wigwam in an hour — "it had no frame, onely a few poles set up together and covered with our boates sailes."

[2] Thornton's Landing at Cape Ann, page 80.

[3] Colonial Soc. of Mass., January, 1908, page 26. Thomas Dudley said that chimneys of wood and roofs of thatch were prohibited in 1630.

His precious books and papers safe from the weather, Blaxton, with the help of Walford and the advice of Maverick, set about the construction of a durable house. He probably built a stout fence or pale which surrounded both the house and the original log shelter, including within its bound the spring and a garden plot, as well as a "run" for his goats or hogs. Maverick tells us that in 1626 there was not a horse or sheep in the country. Even goats and hogs were scarce. A few cows came in 1624.

THOMAS WALFORD'S MARK

Alexander Corbett, writing of Blaxton's life in Boston, says: "The blueberry and blackberry bushes that covered Beacon hill helped to supply his frugal table, as did wild strawberries and grapes, which were close at hand in their season, while the wild roses through which he waded whenever he went abroad would permeate his little cuddy-house with delightful fragrance.

"For a small trinket bestowed now and then among the Indians that inhabited the opposite shores, he could always be supplied with oysters, clams and other fish that abounded almost at his very door, and Indian corn, smoked or dried fish, lobsters and venison for winter's store, could be obtained with equal facility."

In the same year Mr. Maverick built his house opposite the north end of Boston in what is now Chelsea. It was then called Winnesimmet. He says that it had a "Pillizado and fflankers and gunnes both belowe and above." This suggests a larger house than Blaxton's.

A short distance up the Mystic River the third settler in the Bay to leave Wessagusset, Thomas Walford the blacksmith, built a palisaded and thatched house for his family. These men, bound together by the ties of a common experience, were members of the Church of England. Maverick and Blaxton were gentlemen to whom Walford's skill must have been invaluable in the repair of tools, weapons of defence, and domestic hardware. Maverick was a trader in furs and a successful man of business. Blaxton, fond of flowers and fruit, a lover of woodland and sea, surely found these experiences of the summer of 1625 very enjoyable.

During the year 1626, perhaps in the autumn, David Thomson came from Piscataqua with his wife and son to settle on an island opposite the mouth of the Neponset River and east of the Dorchester peninsula. He had been a merchant at Plymouth in Devon, and had come in the spring of 1623 to "Little Harbor" on the west side of and near the mouth of the Piscataqua River. There he had built a "strong and large house," enclosed by a high palisade and protected by guns.[1] After three years of life at Little Harbor he came to the Bay to end his days.

---

[1] "Little Harbor," Thomson's settlement, is now Odiorne's Point in the town of Rye.

If "Caribdis underneath the mould" of Morton's poem in the "New English Canaan" (page 277), written for the May pole revels in 1627, represents David Thomson, and "Scilla sollitary on the ground" is Amias, his widow, then Thomson was dead before May, 1627. The new husband lacking "vertue masculine" is of course Samuel Maverick, said to have been as strong as Samson and as patient as Job. And she was, according to Morton, a difficult "Dallila"; but she was an heiress after Thomson's death, and suitors came by water from all about the Bay to pay their court to her. Mrs. Thomson was the daughter of William Cole of Plymouth, England. Perhaps her second marriage which prevented her return to England caused her father to threaten to deprive her of her property.[1]

AMIAS MAVERICK

Although there were very few white women in Boston harbor at this time, Edward Johnson's description of the hardships endured later by pioneers may serve to complete the picture of those days. He wrote: "The valiant of the Lord waited with patience, and in the misse of beere supplied themselves with water, even the most honoured as well as others,

---

[1] Her letter from Noddles Island, dated 20 November, 1635, asks Robert Trelawny to help her. — *Trelawny Papers,* page 76.

contentedly rejoycing in a Cup of cold water, blessing the Lord that had given them the taste of that
living water, and that they had not the water that
slackes the thrist of their naturall bodies, given them
by measure, but might drinke to the full; as also in
the absence of Bread they feasted themselves with
fish, the Women once a day, as the tide gave way, resorted to the Mussells, and Clambankes, which are a
Fish as big as Horse-mussells, where they daily gathered their Families food."

The winters at Shawmut must have been long and
somewhat dull, although Mr. Blaxton had his books
as a solace.  If, as seems the case, he acted as the
agent of the Gorges family at Shawmut, he must have
watched the drift of current happenings with lively
interest.  We know that he had a Pequot squaw who
did his housework, and he probably had a man also
if his grant of land at Muddy River "for three heads"
refers to the number in his home.  In 1637 Governor
Winthrop reported to Roger Williams at Providence
that runaway servants from Boston were supposed
to have gone past Williams's place in their flight.
Williams replied on November 10th that two Pequot
squaws had been brought to his house in a starving
condition by the Narragansetts.  He had promised
that if they would not run away again he would write
to Boston to ask if they could not be used kindly.  The
bigger girl had worked at "Mr. Coles's," probably
Samuel Coles's tavern, where she was "the worst used
of all natives in Boston," being beaten with fire sticks

by other servants. The morals of his place were disgraceful. The smaller squaw with no grievance had run away from Winnesimmet (which Mr. Maverick had recently left) in company with Mr. Blaxton's squaw. The passage in Williams's letter is confused, but it would seem that when Maverick left Winnesimmet in 1634–35 and Blaxton left Shawmut in 1635 these two girls who had become friends, just as their masters were friends, became unhappy and ran away to the Pequot nation. The Winnesimmet girl fell in with Coles's girl and they were taken to Mr. Williams. The Blaxton girl reached Nayantick, now Westerly, Rhode Island, on the Connecticut border, where the Pequots lived.

Let us imagine Mr. Blaxton in and about his home, devoting part of the day to study, and when the weather was fine, spending some hours in a walk about Shawmut. If the air was clear he could mount West Hill, back of his house, going by a path through the bushes, first marked out, perhaps, by wandering animals, and more clearly marked by his own steps. Once at the top he could see the smoke from Mr. Maverick's chimney, or from galley fires of fishing fleets halting on their way to the Grand Banks. It was no uncommon sight for the white sails of these craft to be visible from West Hill or the more easterly end of the great ridge.

Another walk was along the southern side of the ridge to the little cove at Dock Square. Standing here, Mr. Blaxton could look far down the harbor.

On one such walk in the spring of 1627 Blaxton may have seen a shallop coming into the harbor from Cape Ann. Her master was Captain John Fells, who had come in Captain Johnston's larger ship[1] with Irish settlers for Virginia; the ship had gone ashore at Chatham during the preceding fall, proving a total loss, and the passengers had been received at Plymouth where they spent the winter. Fells was an ardent churchman and also a man of easy habits; he soon met difficulties in his new surroundings, and gossip was rife. Some did not care for his religion, but more were troubled by his evident regard for the young woman who kept his house in order. When he left Plymouth for Cape Ann and the Bay in search of transportation to Virginia, he carried his maidservant with him. They were received by Samuel Maverick at Winnesimmet and no doubt found congenial companionship. The settlement at Winnesimmet was in those days as to its standard in morals and drinking mid-way between Plymouth and Merrymount. Maverick himself was a cultivated and able gentleman, but of a convivial nature. The men who served him at his fortified trading post were of the type familiar to readers of Bret Harte's mining town stories. The Indians who camped near the white men were not slow to practice European vices.

Fells, after his visit, returned to Plymouth, and

---

[1] There is a tradition that she was called *The Sparrow-Hawk*. Nathaniel Morton says that Johnston was the captain, although the Minutes of the Council of Virginia (1924), page 118, refer to "a shipp fro Ireland, Mr ffells master," meaning this voyage. Perhaps he was the sailing master. Fells in 1623 was captain of the *Jacob* of 80 tons, but if Morton is correct Fells was not in command on this voyage.

some months later engaged two barks to carry his
company to Virginia. The maidservant visited at
Merrymount for a few weeks and then followed him.
When off Buzzard's Bay, she gave birth to a child
which soon after died. She was, said Morton,
*too good for earth, too bad for Heaven,*
and he who knew her shall be allowed the last word.

Certain facts are brought to light by the incident
that illustrate the leisurely ways of commerce at this
time. Plans for the voyage of Captain Fells must
have been made in the winter of 1624–25, John Hart
agreeing to attend to the disposal of goods and indentured servants once the ship should reach Virginia.
The cargo was to arrive before 25 December, 1625.
By the summer of 1626 the ship had not cleared from
England. In October, 1626, Hart agreed that if Fells
did not arrive by Christmas, 1626, he would pay a
forfeit for failing to deliver a servant to an impatient
planter. Fells and his company did reach Virginia
in the autumn of 1627.[1]

It is probable that religious services were held
from time to time at all the coast settlements. Mr.
Blaxton as a friend and neighbor of Mr. Maverick
must have preached at Winnesimmet. In the winter
of 1629–30 the Rev. Francis Bright officiated there.
His views were in harmony with Maverick's, and his
rough and ready principles must have pleased the
Winnesimmet type of settler. In a certain sermon
Mr. Bright pictured vividly the Christian life until

[1] New English Canaan, Book III, Chapters 9, 13; Bradford's History
(Ford), II, 16; Abstract Proc. Va. Co. of London, volume 2, page 214;
New England's Memorial, year 1627.

his eye fell upon an Indian who wore a very fine beaver coat. Bright at once directed his discourse to covetousness and the sin of trading for beaver skins on the Lord's day. He made a profound impression; but as soon as his audience, still under the spell of his sermon, had dispersed, he drew the Indian into a secluded place and purchased the beaver coat.

Captain Edward Johnson's statement that Maverick was very ready to entertain strangers may suggest that Blaxton was not an entertainer. We do know that he was acquainted with David Thomson, who lived to the east of him, and on occasion listened to the account of his travels and speculations in land. Blaxton must have visited Maverick, "an enemy to the Reformation in hand," as he was called, whose views on non-conformity and the Separatist doctrine were never concealed from those with whom he came in contact. Walford would have visited him to exercise his skill as a mechanic. These men, together with an occasional sea captain bearing the latest news, a wandering Indian begging bread or having a turkey or hare for barter, and now and then a visitor from Wessagusset, Plymouth, or Piscataqua, must have made the winter days pass pleasantly enough. We know that he examined the weather conditions daily and made a record in his diary.

As spring approached the ice broke up and the ground became green. Then his fruit trees which he had pruned during the winter began to come into leaf. The rose bushes which tradition says he had

came into bud, to send their fragrance later over the fields we now call Boston Common. He no doubt experienced, as did those who came later, "the extreame parching heate of the Sun (by reason of a more constant clearnesse of the Aire then usually is in England)" which scorched the herbs and fruits. We can imagine Mr. Blaxton, for he was a young man still, busy with his planting, his pruning, his hoeing and the feeding of his stock. Beef and pork, brought from England and Ireland, were very expensive, but venison was obtainable. It is probable that he, as soon as possible after 1626, had his cow, pigs and chickens.

Spring brought activity in the Bay and news of varying interest. The Rev. John Lyford, who had been grubbing along at Natascot (Hull) after his expulsion in 1624 from Plymouth, moved over the water to Cape Ann (1625) and to Naumkeag (1626).

The next year he listened to a call to settle in Virginia, where he died. His will was proved May 19, 1632. His contemporaries, Conant and the Virginians, thought well of him but Bradford did not like him, and with Winslow's help gave him a bad name in history. As late a writer as the author of "The Founding of New England" bears testimony to the hypnotic influence of Bradford when he refers to Lyford (page 107) in language wholly inapplicable to his character.

In the spring of 1627 Thomas Morton's celebrations at Mt. Wollaston (Quincy), where he and his followers — lawless traders — set up a May pole, drank heavily, and danced with Indian women, came to the notice of the Bay settlements. The camp was broken up by Standish.

David Thomson's death was an event near home and must have called for Mr. Blaxton's ministrations and sympathy. All we know of this sad event is the simple statement that Mrs. Thomson, *not* Mr. Thomson, gave money to the Plymouth expedition under Standish to arrest Morton, and once for all suppress the scandals at his place called Merrymount.

If the "Rev. Mr. Rogers" of Bradford's *History* who came to New Plymouth in the spring of 1628 was "Mr. Bubble" of *The New English Canaan* we learn from a marginal note that his name was John, perhaps admitted to Clare College 1616, B.A. 1620–21, M.A. 1624, ordained 1625–26. Mr. Bubble was a big-boned man, a scholar interested in the Indian language, and knew shorthand. He was a dull preacher and fond of long prayers. He was called by Morton "This mazed man"; and Morton's stories show that Rogers was "crased in his braine" as Bradford wrote. He was moreover anxious to make money but was too poor a sportsman to prosper at hunting. Mr. Bubble served as "master of ceremonies" and "house chaplain" at Plymouth when Oldham was absent, that is, during the winter of 1628–29 when. Rogers was there. His interest in the language of the Indians would explain why Isaac Allerton brought Rogers over at the Company's expense.

Morton, as was his custom, went out one day in his canoe to Nut Island, near Peddock's Island, to shoot brant geese, and took Rogers with him. The clergyman could not paddle or row well enough to pick up the wounded geese and Morton in disgust brought him home. Morton also tells at some length the tale of Rogers's expedition to the present Worcester county for beaver skins. The minister at night deserted his Indian guides and wandered for days amid the brambles with his legs naked and his breeches tied over his head. We must agree with Bradford that it was advisable to send him back to England.

*Thomas Morton*

THOMAS MORTON

During the year 1628 the "Dorchester Company" sent a colony to Naumkeag (later called Salem) to settle under a patent purchased by John Endecott and others. Matthew Cradock was Governor and Roger Ludlow was deputy governor. John Endecott was selected to act as advance agent for the Dorchester Company and after he sailed he was chosen "governor." With his wife and 20 or 30 other settlers he went from Weymouth in the *Abigail* 20 June, 1628, arriving at Naumkeag on September 6th. Endecott was a vigorous administrator, and as governor or manager had much to do since he could see danger in such a variety of menaces as the Prayer Book, tobacco, the Cross of St. George of the British flag, and the revelries of Thomas Morton at Merrymount. He exercised authority under the English council until Winthrop arrived as "governor" 12 June, 1630, with a charter which, being transferred, carried the government to New England. Endecott could not subscribe to that amiable dictum of Hubbard's that "the difference of men's principles ought to be imputed to the weakness of their natures [rather] than the wickedness of their vices."

Meanwhile the Robert Gorges patent of 1622, extending from Boston Harbor to Nahant, under which Blaxton lived, was superseded by that of the Dorchester Company of 1628, which extended from three miles south of the Charles River to three miles north of the Merrimac. In 1629 Blaxton with William Jeffreys, as attorneys for John Gorges, transferred part of the Robert Gorges grant to John Oldham. The futile transaction is of importance only as it gives us a glimpse of Blaxton. He, with William Jeffreys and Edward Hilton, acted as attorney to transfer land between Cape Elizabeth and Cape Porpoise (the grant of 28 February, 1629) to Thomas Lewis and Richard Bonython. Sir Ferdinando Gorges and John Mason still held "the Province of Maine" from the Merrimac to the Kennebec by a grant of 10 August, 1622.

On the 12th of July, 1630, Winthrop and Dudley arrived in Boston Harbor where Mr. Maverick, "a man of very loving and courteous behaviour, very ready to entertaine strangers," received them. Many of the women and children remained in Salem, while the men put up tents and huts at Charlestown and organized a government and church.

# VII

## OUTPOSTS OF EMPIRE

BEFORE continuing the story of Mr. Blaxton and his neighbors, a word must be said about the greater world of which they were a part. Indeed they were little more than puppets at the far end of threads held in the hands of great London noblemen. These titled lords were adventurers for profit all along the coast; and by the time Mr. Blaxton was well settled at Shawmut they had sent their colonies to Newfoundland, so well described in Captain Edward Wynne's letters, to Bermuda where Norwood's map shows the houses and forts of the settlers, to St. Kitts and Barbados. Indeed there were hundreds of men in Maine and New Hampshire in 1626, or more than double the number of those in Massachusetts. Virginia and Barbados each had six times as many as were round about Blaxton. Even a decade later, when those masters of colonizing propaganda, the New England Puritans, numbered some twenty thousand, the southern colonies had three times as many pioneers. It has been our habit to look upon the Puritan leaders of the North as religious exiles who burned with zeal for a righteous cause. Every such claim has its seeds of truth, but it must not be forgotten that the early "governors," Conant, Endecott and Winthrop, were at first merely local

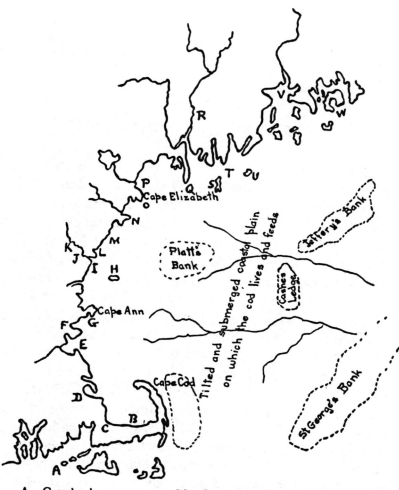

A. Cuttyhunk
B. Weymouth
C. Merrymount
D. Plymouth
E. Boston Harbor
F. Salem
G. Gloucester (Cape Ann)
H. Isles of Shoals
I. Little Harbor
J. Portsmouth
K. Dover
L. York

M. Cape Neddick and Savage Rock
N. Saco (Winter Harbor)
O. Richmond Island, off Cape Elizabeth
P. Casco Bay
Q. Popham Beach
R. Kennebec River
S. Damerill's Isles
T. Pemaquid Point
U. Monhegan
V. Penobscot Bay and River
W. Mt. Desert

managers of English trading companies whose resident members were few in number.

Let us then make a rapid survey of the coast settlements at about the year 1626.

The Rev. William Blaxton was living on the southern slope of Beacon Hill, at what we call the western corner of Beacon and Spruce Streets. He had come from Wessagusset in 1625, and remained in Boston until 1635, when he settled in Rhode Island. His home at Study Hill was then in New Plymouth Colony, and was later found to be in the state founded by Roger Williams.

Samuel Maverick was at Winnesimmet (Chelsea). He, too, had come from Wessagusset in 1625. In 1634 he moved to Noddles Island, where he kept open house for travelers. He was in New York in 1664.

Thomas Walford had a fortified house at Mishawum (Charlestown), and had come from Wessagusset in 1625. In 1631 he was banished, and settled in Portsmouth, New Hampshire. Meanwhile the Sprague family and some settlers of the 1628 migration came over from Salem to develop Charlestown.

David Thomson came to Thompson's Island, from Little Harbor, Piscataqua, in 1626. He seems to have died the same year, leaving a widow who married Samuel Maverick, and a son John whose claim to the Island was recognized in 1648.

Thomas Morton and Captain Wollaston were at Pasonagesset or Mt. Wollaston (Quincy), having come from England about 1625 with three or four gentlemen and thirty men who had sold their time. Morton became a picturesque figure against the drab Pilgrim background.   He was arrested as a roysterer in 1628 and sent to England, but returned.  His "New English Canaan" refers to his life.  Captain Wollaston took with him to Virginia most of Morton's companions before the enterprise had been fairly started.

William Jeffreys, John Bursley and others were at Wessagusset (Weymouth), from England in 1623. Most of the "six gentlemen and divers men to do their labor" had faded away by 1626, but two or three forceful leaders remained.   This colony, in spite of varying fortunes, survived as a prosperous Bay town, and was so favored as to have the late Charles Francis Adams for its historian.

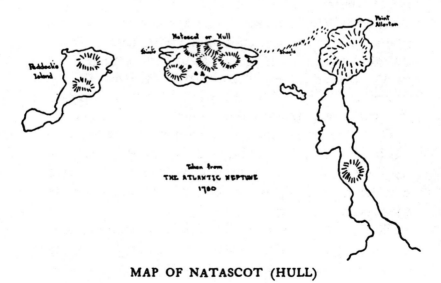

MAP OF NATASCOT (HULL)

John Gray and John Oldham were at Natascot with a few fishermen and stragglers. Natascot (Pemberton Landing) was then an island. In 1644, having 20 houses and a minister, it was named Hull, and the name Nantasket was transferred to the famous beach beyond Point Allerton. It was at this time a place of refuge for those who did not like the Separatist doctrine.

With Conant at Naumkeag (Salem) are said to have been Rev. John Lyford, John Balch, Peter Palfrey, Richard Norman and son, William Allen, Thomas Gray, John Woodbury, John Tylly, Thomas Gardner, William Trask, and for a short time William Jeffreys. The arrival of Endecott in 1628 changed the whole atmosphere of the settlement, although a distinct attempt was made to placate these "old planters." Higginson in 1629 said that he found, on arrival, "half a score houses built, and a fayre house newly built for the governour," this being Conant's house, removed from Cape Ann to Salem.

The fishing company at Cape Ann, composed of Dorchester (England) men, had been given steady support by the Rev. John White, author of the "Planter's Plea," but had failed in 1625, with a loss of £3,000 to its promoters. It was a combined agricultural and fishing enterprise. The site was too far from the fishing grounds and the land was poor. Perhaps, also, it was not a position easy of defence, although early maps show that the end of Cape Ann

was an island at that time.  For a short period, however, it was a well-known meeting place for ships, and
here Captain Martin, a passenger on his way to
Virginia, had a sprightly exchange of words with
Humphrey Rastell, a merchant whose unfair treatment of the Captain was not an unusual subject for
discussion in such a port.

The Isles of Shoals have figured largely in our
history, but they seem to have been at this time little
more than a summer fishing station.  Captain Levett
wrote in 1624: "Upon these islands I neither could
see one good timber tree, nor so much ground as to
make a garden."  Captain John Smith touched there
in 1614 and gave the islands his own name.  Phinehas
Pratt of Wessagusset was there in 1622 and 1623 on
fishing trips, and Thomas Morton of Merrymount
was apparently sent there in 1628 to be shipped to
England.  He had to wait for a month before being
taken off.

WILLIAM HILTON

The Piscataqua River was at this time a place of
real importance.  David Thomson, a well-known merchant, had just moved away to his island home in
Boston Harbor, but at Little Harbor, now Rye, New

Hampshire, and at Hilton's Point, now Dover, men
of ability were permanently settled. William Hilton
was an educated merchant who cared not for the life
at Plymouth and had left its borders. Edward Godfrey, a man of influence in these parts, had been interested in the coast as early as 1609, when Richard
Vines and perhaps a Captain Damerill were representing Sir Ferdinando Gorges.

At Winter Harbor, now Biddeford Pool, at the
mouth of the Saco River, Richard Vines had been
fitfully a colonist since the winter of 1616/17. The
huts there must have been poor in the year 1618–19,
for the mutinous crew put ashore by Captain Edward
Rocroft preferred to risk a hazardous voyage in an
open boat northward to Monhegan Island with no
better prospect awaiting them than "bad lodging and
worse fare." Vines and John Oldham had a patent
of the Harbor in February, 1629–30. The spot[1] is
now marked by cellar holes as well as apple and
cherry trees. In recent years Biddeford Pool has had
a considerable fishing fleet and a number of old families engaged in the occupation.

At Richmond Island, near Cape Elizabeth, John
Burges had had a post for some years, it is supposed,
before he made his will there in 1627. Walter Bagnall and John Bray (?) succeeded him in 1628; Bagnall was killed in 1631. John Winter, representing
Trelawny and Goodyear, controlled the island and

---

[1] Winter Harbor is a cove on the tip of the spit of land which encloses
the Pool. Locke in his "Shores of Saco Bay" says that Vines built on
Leighton's Point, a projection into the Pool from the western shore.

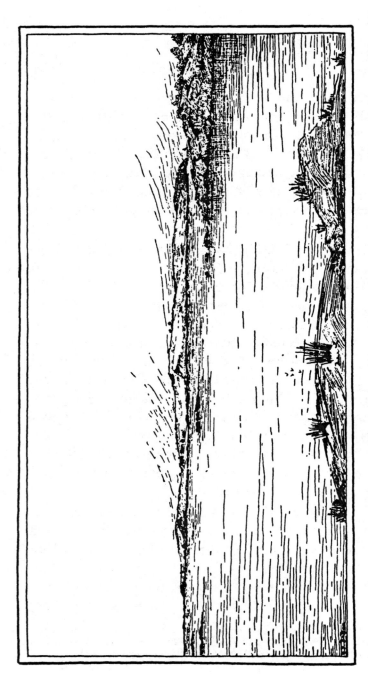

VIEW OF RICHMOND ISLAND

adjoining mainland from that time on for several
years, using the cove on the southwestern shore, which
is fairly well protected. Richmond Island will always hold an important place in the history of fishing because John Winter's letters and accounts are
in print. In one letter still preserved, his story of
Mrs. Winter's troubles with her maidservant covers
four printed pages. "Human interest," therefore, is
not lacking.

Christopher Levett was greatly pleased with Casco
Bay when he arrived in 1623. It was called Quack,
and he proposed to found a city to be named after his
home in York. He put up a building on House
Island, off the shore of South Portland, and sailed
away the next spring, leaving ten men to guard his
treasure. In November, 1627, he said in a letter that
his servants were still there.

In 1627 four men of Weston's ill-founded and ill-
fated colony of Wessagusset were reported to Levett
to be in this house, perhaps by John Winter[1] who put
into the harbor that year, and hired these men in 1630
for work at Richmond Island. George Cleeves and
Richard Tucker in 1630 claimed the mainland at the
mouth of the Spurwink River and opposite Richmond Island but were dispossessed by Winter, representing Trelawny and Goodyear. Cleeves then
settled during 1632 at the present site of Portland
in Casco Bay.

[1] Winter or perhaps Godfrey or Maverick was the man referred to
by Levett in 1627 as "a gent (though a servant of myne in New Eng-
lande)." See Trelawny Papers, page 250.

The famous colony at Popham Beach had come to an end in 1608, but by 1620 or 1630 both sides of the Kennebec there or further up the river had a fleet of fishing ships. A few miles away at Damariscove there was a fishing camp to which ships from Virginia resorted. Here captains and merchants met and talked business soon after the Popham Colony was abandoned. It was referred to often as "Canada." At such meetings servants were, said Mr. Weston, "sold upp & downe like horses." The northern end (Wood End) was in 1780 an island called Wood Island.[1] Damariscove has a small pond near the head of the harbor and a larger one some rods away. In a northeast gale the undertow would carry boats out of the harbor. In good weather fifteen schooners will ride there safely.

Of all these settlements and camps the station at Damariscove is of peculiar note. In the summer of 1622 John Pory, secretary for Virginia, returned to England in the ship *Discovery*. As was the custom, Captain Jones steered for Damerill's Cove; but he touched at New Plymouth, which Pory described in a letter to the Earl of Southampton with freshness and appreciation. In another letter written at about the same time to the governor of Virginia it is significant of conditions in 1622 that he mentions only three settlements on the New England coast. He says:

"Besides that plantation of New Plymouth in 41 degrees and ½, and that other in Massachusett in

[1] See The Atlantic Neptune.

42 or there abouts [apparently Wessagusset, first settled in June of the same year] there is a third in
Canada [*i. e.*, Maine]  At Damrells Cove in 43 and
45 minutes at the cost of Sir Ferd: Gorge, consisting
of some 13 persons who are to p[ro]vide fish all the
yeare with a couple of shallops for the most timelie
·loading of a ship."

It is evident from the above that Damerill's Cove
was an all-the-year-round settlement.  There is still
further evidence of this in Pory's next statement,
copied from Mr. Champlin Burrage's excellent edition of Pory's works:

"To keepe that Iland to be fearmed [farmed] out
in Sir Ferdinandos name to such as shall there fish,
and least [lest] the French or the salvages should
roote them out in winter, they have fortified themselves with a strong pallisado of spruce trees of some
10 foote high, haveing besides their small shott, one
peece of ordinance and some 10 good dogs."

It is not too much to affirm that Damariscove was
from 1608, let us say, to about 1625, the chief mari-
time port of New England.  Here was the rendez-
vous for English, French and Dutch ships crossing
the Atlantic, and for trade between Damariscove and
New Netherland as well as Virginia to the south.
Here men bartered with one another and with Indians, drank, gambled, quarreled, and sold indentured servants.  In other words, the harbor which
a Captain Damerill is assumed to have picked out
years before had by the year 1622 become a typical

commercial seaport on a miniature scale.  In that
year thirty ships rode in the harbor during the fishing
season.

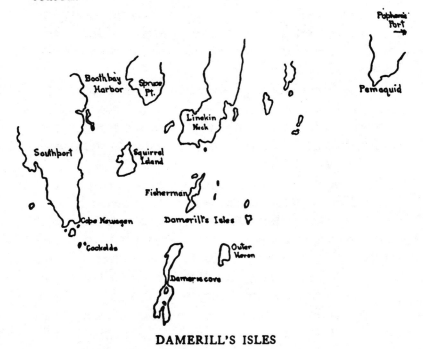

DAMERILL'S ISLES

A century ago the island was covered with a dense
growth of evergreens.  Now only a few gnarled and
picturesque trees cling to the patches of soil, the sheep
having made great havoc with vegetation.  The
northern half of the island, called Wood End, had
trees as late as 1870.  In some places the land is suit-
able for tillage.  There are two weather worn houses,
a dozen shacks and a few sheep sheds near the head

of the harbor. Two hundred yards away lies a fresh
water pond bright in summer with yellow "cow"
lilies and a resort for sea gulls in stormy weather.
Here Captain Kidd is said to have sunk his treasure,
but Dixey Bull the pirate is a more likely aspirant
for the honor. Off the shore, two hundred years after
Captain John Smith's visit, the American brig *Enterprise* and the British brig *Boxer* fought their
famous half hour battle.

Monhegan was probably a more or less permanent
trading post as early as 1614. A fishing village
owned in 1622 by Abraham Jennens was broken up
in 1626, and David Thomson bought some of the fur-
nishings. Jennens sold the island in 1626 to Abraham Shurt, who acted for Aldworth and Elbridge,
Bristol merchants. The harbor is larger than that
at Damariscove, but is not well protected. It has
a sandy bottom but there is a severe undertow in a
northeast gale. Near the beach there is a marshy
or fresh water spot, and to the north there is a pond.

ABRAHAM SHURT

At Pemaquid Abraham Shurt represented Robert
Aldworth and Gyles Elbridge of Bristol. His men
shot one of the crew of Dixey Bull, the rover and

pirate in 1631. Cellars of very early houses have been unearthed, and the "paved street" so much discussed years ago was undoubtedly a "stage" or platform on which fish were dried. The Spanish ambassador in England in 1610 wrote of English colonies recently established on two large rivers. One of these was the attempt at Popham Beach. The other, if not in Virginia, may have been at Pemaquid.

All the above centres of activity along the coast were, under various patents or grants, Church of England settlements.

In addition to these there was the little colony at New Plymouth, composed, said Smith and Maverick, of Brownists, and saved from Indian extermination, says Mr. Adams, by the show of force made by Shurt, Maverick, Thomson and others. These Brownists, later known as "the Pilgrim Fathers," were in a more accurate sense Separatists, and both their beliefs and temper made them uncomfortable for such as Roger Conant, John Oldham, Rev. John Lyford and other men to get on with. Said the Rev. Francis Higginson off Land's End: "We will not say, as the Separatists were wont to say at their leaving of England, Farewell, Babylon! Farewell, Rome! But we will say, Farewell, dear England! Farewell, the Church of God in England, and all the Christian friends there! We do not go to New England as Separatists from the Church of England; though we cannot but separate from the corruptions in it." Winthrop expressed similar sentiments on leaving England.

VIEW OF DAMARISCOVE HARBOR

Cotton Mather was bewildered that sentiments like these registered so poorly with their later conduct. But it is probable that the long voyage afforded opportunity for discussion and meditation, during which England gradually lost its influence. Some men, however, like the Browns of Salem, remained loyal to Mr. Higginson's creed as expressed above. From this time on the leaders of the Bay Colony and New Plymouth gradually fell into accord and systematically built up a Separatist New England, resorting in their zeal to banishment, confiscation of private property, whipping, clipping of ears; and to achieve this end they opened personal letters and unearthed past indiscretions of men who opposed them. That this separation was not the aim of the Massachusetts Bay Company is shown by the Church of England books given and to be sent to the Colony.

It was inevitable that the northern colonists and the Separatists at Boston and Plymouth should not see eye to eye. Mr. Jenness in his entertaining work on the Isles of Shoals has exposed the gulf between them by contemporary opinions on each side. Thomas Dudley stated that some of his fellow passengers in 1630 proved to be "desperately wicked" and were drawn away to the Piscataqua where they had heard of men "of their own disposition." [1] Thomas Jenner in 1640 called the people on the Maine coast "generally very ignorant, superstitious, and vitious, and scarse any religious." [2]  The people

---

[1] Young's Chronicles, page 315.
[2] Mass. Hist. Soc. Coll., series 4, volume 7, page 355.

north of the Merrimac were not too temperate in re-
tort. Captain Underhill of Hilton's Point on the
Piscataqua said in 1638 that the Bostonians were re-
ligiously zealous "as the scribes and Pharisees were,"
and was haled into court for a reprimand.[1] Another
man from the same settlements said in 1632 that the
Massachusetts men "all goe to the Devil; they are a
people not worthy to live on God's earth; fellows that
keep hogs all the week, [and] preach there on the
Sabbath.[2] Perhaps Mr. Jenness is not far wrong
when he adds: "The Character of the New England
Puritan or even of the Separatist of New Plymouth,
is painfully sterile to the fancy, and dreary to the
feelings."[3] This warfare of words between New
Hampshire and Massachusetts is no more to us than
cause for a smile. But in those days it foreshadowed
ill feeling to come. Any one who reads the story of
the crushing out of liberty in the worship of God
when Massachusetts absorbed Maine in 1652 will
have much to think about.

[1] Hubbard's New England, page 353.
[2] Mass. Hist. Coll., series 4, volume 6, page 486.
[3] Isles of Shoals, page 166.

# VIII

## THE BREAK-UP OF THE CHURCH OF ENGLAND COLONY IN THE BAY

WHEN the Puritan settlers at Charlestown, who arrived in 1630, had been reduced in numbers by the ravages of scurvy and had found that the water was poor, they came over in September, 1630, to Shawmut. Their chief men built houses near the present Dock Square and State Street.

In Young's Chronicles it is said that Blaxton "came and acquainted the Governor of an excellent spring there, inviting and soliciting him thither." This generous invitation to the dissenters to invade his privacy has been lauded, and rightly so. If it is true, Blaxton lived to rue the day of his kindness. The assertion was one of many recorded by John Greene of Charlestown in 1664, gathered from survivors of these "first days," and stamped with the approval of the selectmen for entry in the town records. Winthrop had taken over the Gorges rights, and resistance to his coming would have been useless. The solitary settler lived to see the streets of Boston "full of Girles and Boys sporting up and downe, with a continued concourse of people."

Blaxton must have had some intercourse with Governor Winthrop, and with the two early non-conformist clergymen, Wilson and Cotton, who were from the same university and no doubt had points of sympathy. Blaxton may have given some of his apple trees to Governor Winthrop, for in 1638 John Josselyn speaks of good pippins that came from Governor's Island, in the harbor. If we may hazard a guess that the Rev. John Blaxton, "preacher of God's word at Osmington, Dorsetshire," was William's brother, it is conceivable that the Blaxton family became tired of the abuses that had grown up in the state church. John was showing his discontent by printing a remonstrance against clergymen who held several livings and left the work to inferior curates at low pay. Nevertheless, he was incumbent at Osmington as late as 1650, where he had already been for 28 years "a painful minister and orthodox in his doctrines." [1]

We now come to a cryptic statement in Johnson's "Wonder-Working Providence":

"All this while little likelihood there was of building the temple for God's worship, there being only two that began to hew stones in the mountains, the one named Mr. Bright and the other Mr. Blaxton, and one of them began to build; but when they saw all sorts of stones would not fit in the building, as they supposed, the one betook him to the Seas againe and the other to till the land, retaining no symbol of his former profession but a Canonicall Coate."

This has been treated so well by Dr. De Costa that I quote his words:

"Bright, it appears, was a clergyman of the Church of England, who had come out with the people, but was disliked, as Hubbard shows. Morton, in his Memorial (p. 93, ed. 1826),

[1] Hutchinson's Dorset, volume 2, page 509.

says distinctly that Bright 'was a conformist.' Evidently he had credited the people of the *Arbella* with sincerity when they declared that they were misjudged by those who said that they meditated separation.   Bright came, like the Browns, expecting to enjoy a free Church in a free State.   The Browns at Salem reproached Skelton and Higginson for their course, and were put on board a ship and sent home to England.   Bright, however, was more careful, and came to Charlestown with a part of the company, evidently hoping to hold them somewhat to the Church.   Mather says that Blackstone and Bright 'began to hew,' while Bright himself 'began to build.'   His efforts, nevertheless, proved in vain. He could not keep them to their promises, while Blackstone would not join 'the Church.' "

William Blaxton, who always wore his ecclesiastical garb, was admitted a freeman 18 May, 1631. Maverick said that this could only be done if one would "acknowledge the discipline of the Church of England to be erroneous and to renounce it." Cotton Mather wrote of Blaxton: "This man was, indeed, of a particular humor, and he would never join himself to any of our churches, giving this reason for it: 'I came from England because I did not like the *lord bishops;* but I can't join with you because I would not be under the *lord brethren.*' " Two years later the authorities granted Blaxton 50 acres of land to be laid out near his house, and to be his forever. In 1634 he released all but six acres of this concession, and these 43¾ acres became the common or public field for training and pasturage. John Odlin when 70 years old testified that each householder paid 6 shillings "and some more" toward the purchase of this land.

It would seem to me possible that Blaxton was made the first freeman as a courtesy or that he conformed to the views of those in power merely to get his house in order for removal to a more congenial government. In any case, events followed soon upon his becoming a freeman. He sold his land in 1634 or 1635 to Richard Pepys, gentleman, of Boston (he called it Peeps), who built a house thereon.[1] It is evident that William Pollard and his wife Anne lived in this new house for 14 years as employees or gardeners for Pepys, who may himself have taken over the Blaxton house. Mrs. Pollard in her deposition in 1711 says that Blaxton frequently "resorted" to their house, probably on his visits to Boston in later life. No doubt she ate some of his sweet apples. His trees bore a good crop from season to season, and in 1646 Parson Danforth picked them on August 12th, as he records in his diary.

Blaxton, it was deposed by Robert Walker and William Lytherland, used the money which he obtained from the sale of his land to buy cattle. The same year, 1635, on April 7th he obtained a court judgment that Nahanton, an Indian, should pay him two beaver skins for damage done to his swine by setting traps.

Thus he was ready for his great trek. Gathering his books and manuscripts, furniture, cattle, swine, rose bushes and flower seed, he moved with his servants along the trail which led to a hill near Paw-

[1] In 1643 the town considered whether to sell land towards Mr. Blaxton's beach to Mr. Pepys.

STUDY HILL IN 1877

122

tucket. The site when bought from the Indians was called Rehoboth North Purchase or Attleborough Gore, and was at that time in the northwest corner of Plymouth Colony, although Blaxton claimed that he lived in the Bay Colony. It is now in the village of Lonsdale in the town of Cumberland, Rhode Island, three miles north of Pawtucket, and six from Providence.[1] There was no road until 1650. He did not hold a deed to this land, but in 1671 Plymouth Colony granted 200 acres where he then lived.

He settled close to a fordway near a bend on the east bank of the Pawtucket River. This was a spot frequented by the Indians and known to them as "Wawepoowseag," or the place where birds are ensnared. His home, which he called Study Hill, was 60 or 70 feet above the river and, said Mr. Thomas C. Amory, commanded a fine view of the valley of the Blackstone to the distance of more than a mile. "On the east is another delightful and fertile valley which opens to the south on the borders of the meadow." Here he built a cottage in a meadow four rods east of his "Study hill top," having first dug a cellar and walled it with stone. South of the cellar he dug a well in a second terrace or meadow a little lower down toward the river. Below this level was a third meadow. He planted his orchard at the south end of his meadow, and these trees were said by Governor Hopkins in 1765 to be "still pretty thrifty fruit-

---

[1] "Three miles above Pawtucket and a mile and a half above Valley Falls on the west side of the stage road from Pawtucket to Worcester." Later the Whipple place. The mill of the Lonsdale Manufacturing Company now occupies the site (Crane).

bearing trees." They were called yellow sweetings. Three trees were still standing in 1836. When Blaxton rode to Providence to preach he had on the first occasion, it is said, an audience of one man, two women, and a number of children whom he collected by throwing apples to them.[1] As his audience increased he was wont to carry apples in his saddlebag for the children, for whom he had a great affection. At the time of Blaxton's death there were 160 inhabitants in the neighborhood of his home. It is not unreasonable to suppose that he preached at times to these people. Tradition says that he had a servant or man of all work named Abbot. For him the brook which enters the Blackstone River just below Valley Falls was named Abbot's Run.

It seems clear that Blaxton visited his friends or traveled on business from time to time. On one of those occasions when he came to Boston and stayed with Mr. Pepys, or possibly with the Pollards, he had a grant of land at Muddy River (now Brookline, Mass.) "for three heads." This allotment was to the inhabitants of 1635. The record would indicate that two persons had been living with him. Either Blaxton delayed his removal from Boston until after this grant or, what seems more probable, he was entitled to this grant of land by virtue of his position as a freeman and because of property owned in Boston previous to his departure. No deeds bearing his name exist.

[1] Ezra Stiles's Literary Diary, volume 1 (1901), page 186.

Blaxton returned to Boston frequently, as has been said. On one of these visits he married at Boston, 4 July, 1659, Sarah, the widow of John Stevenson, who lived on the southwest side of Milk Street on a site where later Benjamin Franklin was born. Mrs. Stevenson was at that time the mother of several children mentioned in the Boston records. One at least, John, survived to be a consolation to his mother and stepfather in their declining years.

Governor Endecott performed the marriage. Blaxton was then 63, and a bachelor. If Boston was too populous for one of his tastes, the new home at Study Hill had proved itself to be too lonely. This surprising marriage could be made the theme for endless contemplation. He no doubt needed a housekeeper, and it was best then, as it is the custom now, for a man and woman living on an isolated farm to be married. The one tangible fact is that Blaxton became the father of a son, born about 1661, whom he named John. This son eventually settled near New Haven, and his descendants rose to some prominence. Their genealogy has been published.

We get glimpses of this first inhabitant of Shawmut or Boston after his removal to Rhode Island. He lived on what might be called a forest thoroughfare and therefore had occasional callers, both white and Indian. A year or more after his settlement Roger Williams came to be his neighbor. They had become freemen the same day, 18 May, 1631. Williams had preached in Salem and had questioned the authority of the magistrates.  He was banished in October or November, 1635, and came in the summer of 1636, after many vicissitudes, to live in a place

ROGER WILLIAMS

which he called Providence.  He and Blaxton there-fore were neighbors and continued tolerant of one another's views.

A year or two later Thomas Lechford paid Blaxton a visit and said that "he lives neere master Williams but is far from his opinions."  They must have found much pleasure in the exchange of books from their libraries.  Blaxton had, besides three Bibles, and his ten manuscript volumes, six large books in Latin and six in English, as well as 159 smaller works.

With perhaps some approach to imagination, it is recorded how he used to visit Richard Smith at "Smith Castle," Narragansett, later the town of Wickford.  The poet has said:

> He loved his books, but nature too;
> Explored the country wild,
> Mounted upon his cream-white steed
> Submissive as a child.

The ford at the Pawtucket River, by Blaxton's house, was on the highway from New London to Boston.  The path followed the shore of Long Island

Sound from the mouth of the Connecticut River east-
ward through New London, Westerly, and up the
west shore of Narragansett Bay through Wickford
to Roger Williams's house at Providence. Then it
passed Blaxton's house and went by Walpole or
Sharon to Boston. Smith kept a tavern and carried
on, as Williams said, a "bloody liquor trade" which
made devils of the Indians in spite of the efforts for
peace by him and Blaxton.

Blaxton had two powerful Indian friends in Rhode
Island, Miantonomo, a nephew of Canonicus, king
of the Narragansetts, and Ousamekin, better known
as Massasoit, who was king of the Wamponoags.
These chiefs, and the two sons of the latter — Ca-
nonchet and Philip — lived in peace with the whites
until Blaxton's death, no doubt a tribute to his gentle,
conciliatory spirit which made it possible for him
to dwell with Puritan and savage alike.

Blaxton, with his wife Sarah, his son John, and his
stepson John Stevenson, lived at Study Hill for a
dozen years in peace and prosperity until Mrs. Blaxton died in June, 1673. He stayed on with his children until his own death on 26 May, 1675. Williams, writing from Richard Smith's house at Wickford 13 June, 1675, to Governor Winthrop of Connecticut, makes this statement: "About a fortnight
since your old acquaintance, Mr. Blackstone, de-
parted this life in the fourscore year of his age; four
days before his death he had a great pain in his
breast, and back, and bowels; afterward he said he

was well, had no pains, and should live, but he grew fainter, and yielded up his breath without a groan."

When Blaxton became ill it is reasonable to suppose that Roger Williams, six miles away, was called to his bedside, and no doubt he remained there until Mr. Blaxton died.

Blaxton was buried 28 May, 1675, and his grave was marked by "two plain whitish oval bowlders, one at the head and the other at the foot, rising but a few inches above the ground." The site was two rods east of the knoll which he called Study Hill, on the east bank of the river, and near the railway station. In 1886 only a few bones and coffin nails could be found. In the Indian military operations of the next year the house was destroyed. Mr. Blaxton left 260 acres of land, two shares in "Providence meadows," and the "Blackstone meadows." The court of Plymouth granted 50 acres of the estate and five acres of meadow to John Stevenson because he "was very helpful to his father and mother in their life time, and he is now left in a low and mean condition and never was in any [way] recompensed for his good service aforesaid, and if (as it is said at least) his father in law engaged to his mother at his marriage with her that he should be considered with a competency of land out of the said Blackstone's land, then lived on."

Stevenson lived alone and unmarried on the estate until his death in 1695. John Blaxton lived beside him until he sold the home in 1692 to David Whipple, and moved to Providence where he worked as a shoemaker. By his wife Katharine he had a family, well known and prosperous, near New Haven.

The subsequent history of two other members of the Bay colony should be recorded here since both knew Blaxton well.

SAMUEL MAVERICK

Samuel Maverick of Winnesimmet was the son of the Rev. John Maverick,[1] who crossed the sea a nonconformist in 1630 and served as the minister of Dorchester until his death in 1635/6. The son, here in 1623, came up from Wessagusset, as has been related, and settled at Winnesimmet, now Chelsea, where on 17 June, 1630, he entertained Winthrop. In December, 1633, he, his wife and servants cared for Indians dying of the smallpox, and buried as many as thirty in a single day. In 1634 he moved over to Noddles Island, which had been granted to him in April, 1633. There he built a house and entertained hospitably, as John Josselyn recorded in July, 1638. He was a staunch churchman and loyal to the King. Charles II appointed him with others in 1664 to settle the affairs of New England and New Netherland. He had a house on the Broadway, New York, and died there between 1670 and 1676. In 1660 he wrote a Description of New England,[2] in

[1] N. E. Hist. Gen. Reg., April, 1915, page 153.
[2] N. E. Hist. Gen. Reg., volume 39, page 33.

which he has this to say about the treatment of the
Old Planters by the Puritans:

"This Governo[r] and his Councill, not long after their Aryvall
made a law that no man should be admitted a Freeman, and soe
Consequently have any voyce in Election of Officers Civill or
Military, but such as were first entered into Church covenant and
brought Certificate of it, let there Estates,. and accordingly there
portion of land be never soe great, and there taxes towards publick
Charges.[1]   Nor could any competency of Knowledge or inoffen-
sivenesse of liveing or conversation usher a man into there Church
ffellowship, unless he would also acknowledge the discipline of
the Church of England to be erroneous and to renounce it, which
very many never condescended unto, so that on this account the
far great Number of his Majesties loyall subjects there never in-
joyed those priviledges intended by his Royall ffather in his Grant.
And upon this very accompt also, if not being Joyned in Church
ffelowship many Thowzands have been debarred the Sacrament
of the Lords Supper although of Competent knowledg, and of
honest life and Godly Conversation; and a very great Number
are unbaptized. . . .

"And whereas they went over thither to injoy liberty of Conscience, in how high a measure have they denyed it to others there,
wittnesse theire debarring many from the Sacraments spoken of
before meerly because they cannot Joyne with them in their
Church-ffellowship; nor will they permitt any Lawfull Ministers
that are or would come thither to administer them.   Wittness also
the Banishing so many to leave their habitations there, and seek
places abroad elswhere, meerly for differing in Judgment from
them as the Hutchinsons and severall families with them, & that
Honb[le] Lady the Lady Deborah Moody and severalls with her
meerly for declareing themselfes moderate Anabaptists, Who found
more favour and respect amongst the Dutch, then she did amongst
the English.   Many others also upon the same account needless to
be named.   And how many for not comeing to theire assemblies

---

[1] Governor Dudley told the Countess of Lincoln, 28 March, 1631, that
of about 700 who came in the 17 Winthrop ships in July and August, 1630,
"not much less than a hundred (some think many more)" had moved away
through dislike of the government or fear of famine.

have been compelled to pay 5ˢ a peece for every Sabbath day they misse, besides what they are forced to pay towards the mantenance of the Ministers. And very cruelly handled by whipping and im- prissonment was Mʳ Clark, Obadiah Holmes, and others for teaching and praying in a private house on the Lords day. These and many other such like proceedings, which would by them have been judged Cruelty had they been inflicted on them here, have they used towards others there; And for hanging the three Quakers last yeare I think few approved of it."

That Maverick was not expelled is due no doubt to his social position, his father's prominence as a clergyman, and perhaps in some measure to his genial nature.

Thomas Walford, Blaxton's neighbor at Mishawum, was warned in 1631 with his wife to depart out of the limits of the Bay patent before the 20th of October on pain of confiscation of his goods, for his contempt of authority and confronting officers. His goods were soon sequestered to satisfy claims of reputed creditors. He moved to Portsmouth, where he was much respected, serving on the grand jury in 1654, and as a church warden. His death occurred in 1660.

In 1656 an incident became public gossip which in any later age would have been laughed out of court. Mrs. Susannah Trimmings of Little Harbor, Piscataqua (David Thomson's old place) was walking homeward when she heard a rustling in the woods which she at first attributed to swine. "Old goodwife Walford" soon appeared, dressed in a white linen hood tied under her chin, a black hat, a red waistcoat and petticoat. She asked for the loan of a pound of cotton; when Mrs. Trimmings refused, she predicted increasing sorrow and a journey with no end. The sensitive Mrs. Trimmings was then "struck as with a clap of fire on the back" and Mrs. Walford disappeared in the shape of a cat. Mr. and Mrs. Puddington testified that they had seen in their garden a yellowish cat and some cats of other hues, but they could not identify any one of these cats as Mrs. Walford. It was proved that Mrs. Walford was at home when Mrs. Trimmings said that they met. In spite of all this the so-called witch was bound over to the next court. There the case was allowed to sleep, and Mrs. Walford obtained a verdict for five pounds and costs against Robert Couch for slander.[1]

As one looks back upon the careers of the Old Planters of New England they seem to shine out against the background of intolerance and cruelty. The Rev. Mr. Morrell had ecclesiastical powers that could have been a menace to New Plymouth, but he never tried to exercise them. Mr. Maverick and Mr. Walford, Mr. Lyford and Mr. Oldham suffered slan-

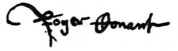

ROGER CONANT

der and did not resort to violence. Roger Conant, the governor of the Dorchester Company settlements, suffered rebuffs without number and bore every af-

[1] N. H. Hist. Gen. Reg., April, 1889, page 181. By J. S. H. Fogg.

front with meekness. He deserves to be remembered. And Mr. Blaxton's Boston should more generously reverence their first inhabitant.

The sixth Article of the Constitution of the United States reads that "no religious test shall ever be required as a qualification to any office or public trust under the United States." This is one of the foundation stones of our Government, and yet it was by no means recognized as just and wise throughout Colonial times. Early Massachusetts Bay and Plymouth could not be brought to take this view, and little by little many of her prominent citizens left to return to England or to settle in Rhode Island, New Hampshire and Maine. Men like Roger Williams pleaded for toleration but there was none. The Old Planters and the fishermen along the coast stood valiantly for the right to hold public office, and to worship each according to his own conscience. Some say that two-thirds, and others say that four-fifths of the male population was disfranchised. These Old Planters, traders, and fishermen were the leaven which brought Massachusetts, and eventually the whole United States, to the principle that the right to individual conscience in religion must not be a bar to participation in government.

MAP OF MONHEGAN

# IX

## THE COLONIZING MIND

IT was on the third of November, 1620 — before the Pilgrims had landed in Plymouth Harbor — that James, by the Grace of God, King of England &c., upon the humble petition of divers well disposed subjects, including Sir fferdinando Gorges, Knight, captain of the fort and island of Plymouth, and other persons of quality, determined to make them a distinct body. They had already — and this is important — been at great and extraordinary charge to seek and discover a place fit and convenient to lay the foundation of a hopeful plantation, and for "*divers years past*" had taken actual possession of the Continent [from Philadelphia to the peak of Maine] and had, as the patent says, "*settled already some of our people in places agreeable to their desires in those parts.*" This shows that there were settlements earlier than that at Plymouth, made by men of the English race.

The petitioners were to establish fisheries, trade, and plantations, named in this order. The charter next refers to the "wonderfull plague" that had depopulated the whole territory, a statement that would seem to be based on the news conveyed by Richard Vines of Saco to Gorges, and by him to the hand that drew up the patent. The land was to be called "by

LARRABEE'S PALISADO, CAPE PORPOISE

the name of New-England, in America." Of the
Council for New England, as the governing body
was familiarly to be called, were Sir Francis Pop-
ham, Sir Richard Hawkins, Rawleigh Gilbert, John
Argall, Esq., and a host of titled people, as well as
Sir Ferdinando Gorges.[1]

They were to work for the "reducing and conver-
sion of such savages as remaine wandering in desola-
tion and distress to Civil Societie and Christian Religion, to the enlargement of our own dominions, and
the advancement of the fortunes of such of our good
subjects as shall willingly intresse themselves in the
said imployment." They were described as the Council established at Plymouth in the County of Devon
for the planting, ruling, ordering and governing of
New-England in America.

It is noticeable that the first object of the enterprise
was to be fishing. The search for the Fountain of
Perpetual Youth and the fever for gold had been
abandoned, or given over to the adventurous Span-
iards. For a century this coast had attracted Europe,
and Captain John Smith was intelligent enough to
see that in cod fisheries, rather than precious min-
erals, lay the possibilities of wealth.

The long building first to be erected on a fishing
site was to serve as barracks, storehouse, and place of
revelry. It had near it platforms for drying the fish.
These were sometimes called flakes, but more often
stages, and were to be found wherever the industry

[1] E. Hazard's Historical Collections, 1792, volume 1, page 103.

was successful. We have still a Stage Island off Cape Porpoise near Kennebunkport; another of the same name off Popham Beach; and a third off Biddeford Pool. Stage Neck is at Cape Ann. There is a Stage Cove between the Gurnet and Saquish Point at the entrance to Plymouth Harbor. To the southeast there are Stage Point and Stage Harbor. These names must be survivals from very early days.

Salt was an essential factor in preserving fish, so we find Salt Island in Machias Bay and another outside Cape Ann, near Bass Rocks. "Stage" and "salt" perpetuate the old fishing centres as no work of historical writing possiby could do.

Other evidences of fishing come to mind in the name Fisherman's Island, next to Damariscove, a very early station, and in Bluefish Point on Martha's Vineyard. When we do not find any one of these names on a stretch of the New England coast it may well raise a doubt if fishing was ever a dominant occupation of pioneers who lived there.

Trade was the next object of the colonizing mind as set down in the patent. On the coast we find islands harking back to the fur trade, Seal islands, Beaver Island, and others, but not as many as one might expect. Rum Key, Dram Island, and Folly Island might equally well reflect the early life along the Maine coast, but I fear that they are late names. The subject could easily be pushed too far.

Of special note, however, are two names of islands which carry us back to the very beginning of the

white man's contact with this coast. Clapboard
Island is off Falmouth Foreside in Portland Harbor.
It is well known that the clapboard industry ac-
counted for many cargoes sent overseas; these clapboards were really oak staves for casks and barrels.[1]
It seems to have flourished far to the north, for there
is a Stave Island northeast of Bar Harbor, and another
east of Chebeag in Broad Sound, Harpswell. Here
men of skill and strength must have toiled before
writers of history came to New England. We do not
know their names, but the results of their work appeared in the hold of every ship that buffeted the sea
between Cornwall and Maine.

And what shall we say of the colonizing mind as it
searched the irregular coast for a settlement? Several
purposes at once become evident as we study the plans
of their earliest landfalls.

First, they sought a small plot of arable land protected by water from a sudden attack by Indians.
Usually an island best met these requirements. The
first European settlement in New England, 26 June,
1604, was made on an island in the Saint Croix River
between Maine and New Brunswick, and called by
De Monts "Acadia."

A harbor large enough to shelter in time of storms
their unwieldy little ships of from 20 to 100 tons was
of vital necessity. If it had rocky shores to which a
ship could be moored by throwing a rope around a
tree, all the better.

[1] Bradford's History (Ford), volume 1, page 235, note.

Wood was also essential.  Damariscove was covered with trees, and the northern half was long called
Wood End.   Off Biddeford Pool, where Richard
Vines lived as early as 1616, there is a Wood Island
as well as a Stage Island.   Both names are used again
for islands off Popham Beach.   The kettle could not
be made to boil without firewood.

Fresh water was another necessity.   Cuttyhunk
Island, where Gosnold settled in 1602, had not only
a fresh water pond but an island within the pond, an
ideal situation.   Biddeford Pool ("Winter Harbor")

MAP OF LITTLE HARBOR
PISCATAQUA

had a pond, as did Sabino or Popham Beach. There was also a Pond Island off the Sabino shore. Damariscove had two ponds of fresh water, frequented by sea gulls. There were ponds at Monhegan.

In some cases, as at Little Harbor or Odiorne's Point, the land was a small peninsula protected by an inlet and marshes. Wessagusset was similarly defended. Popham Beach was virtually an island, made so by the Morse River marshes. In this early period grass land for cattle had not come to be a factor in the selection of a habitation.

It is evident that the colonizer of that day, having firmly before him all the conditions to be met, went from headland to headland and from island to island, searching for a defensible small domain, having a good harbor, soil for a garden, firewood, and a supply of fresh water. Once such a site had been secured, preferably near fishing grounds or at the mouth of a great river on which Indians came down to barter in furs, the adventurer built his house and surrounded it by a palisade.

Every pioneer carried dogs with him. These were large and powerful, so that few Indians cared to try issues with them. Captain Pring had two mastiffs on his voyage in 1605, and there were ten dogs at Damariscove in 1622.

From the above, it will be clear that the earliest fishermen, traders and settlers had very little thought for gold and scant desire to Christianize the red men. Indeed the red man was the great overshadowing

THE ISLAND IN GOSNOLD'S POND

menace of colonization. He stayed its onrush until disease decimated the savage tribes. At last the white man's longing for life in new lands swept resistance aside and left the men of Devon, Cornwall and Somerset masters of the coast. In this first quarter of the seventeenth century they had added a new outpost to the dominions of King James and had become the real founders of New England.

# A TENTATIVE LIST OF OLD PLANTERS AND SOJOURNERS IN NEW ENGLAND BEFORE 6 SEPTEMBER, 1628

For names of settlers at Cuttyhunk (1602) and at Popham (1608) see Appendix B.

This list does not include sea captains and sailors. Plymouth colonists have been too thoroughly well catalogued elsewhere to require details here. Those who died the first winter without issue or left very soon were: William Beale, Richard Britteridge, William Button, John Cannon, Robert Carter, Richard Clarke, Thomas English, Moses Fletcher, Edmond Flood, Richard Gardiner, John Goodman, William Heard, William Holbeck, John Hooke, John Langmore, Edmund Margesson, Thomas Morton (*Fortune*), Augustine Nicholas, William Pitt, Solomon Prower, James Rand, John Rigdale, James Steward, Elias Story, Edward Thompson, Edward Tilley, Thomas Tinker, Roger Wilder, Thomas Williams.

A consolidated alphabetical list of passengers by the *Mayflower* (November, 1620), *Fortune* (November, 1621), *Anne* (July, 1623), and *Little James* (July, 1623), will be found in Goodwin's "Pilgrim Republic," pages 297–300. A critical record is in Colonel Banks's "English Ancestry and Homes of the Pilgrim Fathers" (1929).

A similar list of Salem "Old Planters" and a short list of arrivals before 1630 is given in Drake's "Boston" (1856), page 57. A list of arrivals at Salem in 1629 is given in Frank A. Gardner's "Higginson-Skelton Migration." A list of passengers by the *Mary and John,* arriving 30 May, 1630 (before Winthrop came), by Colonel Banks, was printed in the *Boston Transcript,* 15 April, 1929, page 12. See also May 20th, page 12.

When the four pilgrim ships had come in there were in Plymouth, in the winter of 1623–24, excluding seamen, servants, children, the dead, and the absent, about 50 men and 30 women. Not all of these were Separatists, for many like Robert Hicks, although unhappy, remained. There were at Cape Ann, Casco Bay, Damerill's Cove, Monhegan, Natascot, Pemaquid, Piscataqua and Wessagusset at least 75 men and a few women, almost all nominal members of the Church of England. These had come largely from the south and west coasts of England, while the Plymouth group came chiefly from the vicinity of Aldgate Ward, London, half a mile north of the present Bank of England, housed in the lanes and courts off Cornhill and Leadenhall Street. A few had come from Leyden, where they had been settled for about ten years. (Mass. Hist. Soc. Proc., volume 61.)

ADAMS, John. *Fortune,* 1621.

ALDEN, John. *Mayflower,* 1620.

?ALGER, Thomas, at Levett's house at Casco, 1630; Wessagusset, 1622? From Newton Ferrers, Devon. Four of Weston's 1622 party at Casco, 1627. See Badiver, Baker and Rouse.

ALLEN, William, carpenter, Cape Ann, 1624; Naumkeag, 1626; Manchester, 1640?; born Manchester, England, about 1602; died bet. 7 June, 1678, and 26 of 4th mo., 1679. Essex Antiq., September, 1898, p. 135.

ALLERTON, Mr. Isaac. *Mayflower,* 1620.

ANNABLE, Anthony. *Anne,* 1623.

ASTLEY, Edward, about February, 1627/8, "he first went to New England to inhabit"; "a very profane young man" living with the savages; trader on the Penobscot; arrested 1631 for "trading powder and shote with the Indeans" and in October sent to England for trial. He was put in the *Fleet* prison, and later freed upon bond with a caution. Lost at sea on his return from Russia. Some of his servants (date of arrival not known) were John Deacon, Henry Sampson, George Watson, Oliver Callow and James L——. Affidavit (facsimile with signature) in Bradford, vol. 2 (1912), p. 108. Other testimony, Mass. Hist. Soc. Proc., vol. 45, pp. 493–498. Well educated. Probably one of the Edward Astleys of the Norfolk family represented by Lord Hastings. Perhaps he should be called "Mr."

?ATKINS, Thomas, "an early settler" at Sagadahock. Sold land to William Cox.

?BADIVER, John, Wessagusset, 1622?, Casco, 1630.

BAGNALL, Walter, "Great Watt"; came with Thomas Morton, 1624/5; Merry Mount, 1626–1628?; Richmond Island, 1628; patent for the Island, 1631; killed at Richmond Island, 3 October, 1631; "a wicked fellow," said Winthrop, "and sometimes servant for one in the Bay." Goold's "Portland," Chap. II.

?BAKER, Edmund, at Levett's house at Casco, 1630. From Newton Ferrers, Devon. Wessagusset, 1622? Four of Weston's 1622 party at Casco, 1627. See Rouse and Alger.

BALCH, John, Wessagusset, 1623; Cape Ann, 1624; Naumkeag, 1626; Bass River (Beverly), 1639; died June, 1648, aged 69.

BANGS, Edward. *Anne,* 1623.

BARTLETT, Robert. *Anne,* 1623.

BASSETT, William. *Fortune,* 1621.

BAUDEN, Ambrose, of Holberton, Devon, apprentice to Winter at Casco Bay, 1627; sea captain; ferry keeper over Spurwink River, 1658; blind 1670; killed 1675.

BILLINGTON, John. *Mayflower,* 1620.

?BIRD, Thomas, at Scituate 1627. Deane, pp. 8, 221. Date wrong?

BLAXTON, Rev. William, born 1595–96; B.A. Emmanuel College, Cambridge, 1617–18; ordained 1619; M.A. 1621; Wessagusset, 1623; Shawmut, 1625; Study Hill (Lonsdale, R. I.), 1635; died 26 May, 1675. Married late in life and left descendants.

BOMPASSE, Edward. *Fortune,* 1621.

BOND, John, Jr., agreed 22 October, 1622, to go to N. E. as calker. (Council for N. E.)

BRADFORD, Governor William. *Mayflower,* 1620. See Dr. Samuel E. Morison's sketch in Dict. of Amer. Biography, vol. 2.

BRADSHAW, Richard, Spurwink. Sold land there about 1630 on which he had settled "formerly."

BRAY. See BURGES.

BREWSTER, Jonathan. *Fortune,* 1621.

BREWSTER, William, Gent. *Mayflower,* 1620.

BRIDGE, William, of Charlestown, came a youth to N. E.; in petition says he came (*a*) 21 years before; (*b*) with father-in-law, John Oldham; (*c*) when Governor Endecott was in office. If petition is one referred to in Mass. Colon. Records, 1644, for grant of land, he came 1623 with Oldham, but Endecott was not Governor. If Bridge came 1629 with Oldham, he was dead 21 years later. Bridge mar. Mary Oldham who died about 1646, and had Peter, "son of William and Mary," born 11th month, 1643/4; perhaps Samuel; and Mary, wife of John Knight, Jr. Bridge died 1648/9.

BRIGGS, Clement. *Fortune,* 1621.

?BROWN, John, New Harbor in Pemaquid, 1625; bought Muscongus Island 15 July, 1625. See A. Matthews in Col. Soc. of Mass. Proc., vol. 6. C. T. Libby says 1625 deed a forgery (*Boston Herald*, 3 October, 1926). Brown there later.

BROWNE, Peter. *Mayflower*, 1620.

BURCHER, Edward. *Little James*, 1623.

BURGES, John, of Westleigh, Co. Devon, had a trading station at Richmond Island in 1627. Made his will there 11 April, 1627; proved 24 May, 1628, by widow Joanna Burges, alias Bray; sons Robert, John, William. Had a bark *Annes* with her boat, tackling and provisions, his whistle and chain, and his instruments that belonged to the sea. John Bray of Kittery Point may have been here very early. See Waters's "Gleanings," vol. 1, p. 2.

BURSLEY, Mr. John, Wessagusset, 1623; Dorchester, 1631; with Gorges, Jeffreys, *et al.*, had grant on east side of Agamenticus River, 2 December, 1631; Kittery, 1642; Exeter, 1643.

CARVER, Governor John. *Mayflower*, 1620.

CHAPMAN, Mr., a Londoner, came with Gorges to Plymouth in September, 1623, and died 5 months later.

CHILTON, James. *Mayflower*, 1620.

CLARK, Thomas. *Anne*, 1623.

CONANT, Christopher. *Anne*, 1623.

CONANT, Mr. Roger, bapt. East Budleigh, Devon, 9 April, 1592; mar. Sarah Horton November, 1618; arr. "about Feb. 1622/3," perhaps in *Jonathan of Plymouth* with David Thomson; Natascot, 1624; Cape Ann, 1625; same year one Hewes and Standish "grew hot" over a Plymouth fishing stage and Conant made peace; Naumkeag, 1626; superseded by Endecott 6 September, 1628; deputy to General Court, 1634; town surveyor Salem, 1636; house, 1635 (?) Bass River (Beverly) opposite present John Balch house; in fur trade, 1655; asked, 1671, Bass River to be called Budleigh; 4 June, 1671, a planter in N. E. 48 years and 3 months; died 19 November, 1679. His son married Weston's daughter.

COOKE, Francis. *Mayflower*, 1620.

CORBIN (Robert?), at Damariscove, 1624.

CORNISH, Jeffrey, at Damariscove, 1625.

COUSINS, John, sailor, had known Casco River in 1626; born 1596; of North Yarmouth and York; died 1689. Trelawny Papers, p. 239.

?COX, William, had a fishing stage at Pemaquid, 1624? Deed, 1625, referring to him said by C. T. Libby to be a forgery; witness 1635; living 1660. See Libby's Dict., pp. 19–20.

CRACKSTON, John. *Mayflower*, 1620.

CRIBBE (Benjamin?), at Isles of Shoals? 18 shillings due *Mr.* Cribbe on account of Morton's arrest, 1628; Dorchester, 1630/1.

CUSHMAN, Robert. *Fortune*, 1621.

DAMERILL, Capt. of a Devon-Cornwall family; perhaps with Popham colony 1607–08; or with Vines in 1609; at "Damerill's Iles" 1614; fortified Damerill's Cove before 1622. Perhaps the Capt. Damyron who in 1620 took "50 Bridewell vagabonds" to Va. James Damerill, mariner, of Limehouse, Stepney, London, married, 1609, Rachel Clarke and d. overseas in 1631, leaving sons Thomas, Samuel and William (Colonel Banks). Edward Johnson, merchant, executor of his will, was perhaps the man at Wessagusset in 1622, and on the Merrimac River in 1631. Another Edward married Elizabeth Clarke at Stepney in 1611/12. Dameron and Damerill seem to be the same name. Stoke-Damerell is a dock-side parish in Plymouth, Devon.

?DAMERILL, Capt. Humphrey, mariner, of Limehouse, parish of Stepney; perhaps nephew of one of the above; married there in 1629 Sara Minshew; she living in Boston at his death in 1654, with son John. Humphrey captain of *Sea Flower*. Sara, the widow, married, 1654, in Boston, John Hawkins, probably of Stepney. John Damerill was in 1714 at Merriconeag Neck (Harpswell), Maine.

A widow Elizabeth Damerill married at Stepney, 1627, Capt. John Crowther, mariner, benefactor, dead 1659. Another John Crowther was of Strawberry Bank, 1640, and dead in 1652. One was at Newfoundland in 1612.

DE LA NOYE, Phillipe. *Fortune,* 1621.

DEANE, Stephen. *Fortune,* 1621.

DIKE (DIX), Capt. Anthony, came in *Anne* to Plymouth, July, 1623; Cape Ann or Natascot, ?1624; absent from Plymouth, 1627; freeman, Mass., 1631; trading partner, 1630–33, at Blue Point, near Saco, with Conant, Palfrey, and Johnson; captured by alleged pirate, Dixey Bull, 1632; released and reimbursed; master of the *Blessing of the Bay,* 1636; of Salem, 1636; lost in snowstorm off Cape Cod 15 December, 1638.

DOCKETT, Edmund, in June-July, 1624, at Monhegan as factor for Jennings and Cross, Plymouth merchants. (Libby's Gen. Dict., p. 2.)

DOTY, Edward. *Mayflower,* 1620.

DUGDEALE, George, tailor, offers, 30 November, 1622, to go to N. E. (Council for N. E.)

EATON, Francis. *Mayflower,* 1620.

EDWARDS, William, came to N. E. spring 1624 in *Charity* "and remained there". Deposed by Stephen Bolton of Wapping 12 May, 1625. P. R. O. Admiralty Exams. (Col. Banks.) Man of same name at Richmond Island 1639. Another at Hartford 1646.

?ELLFORD, John, Roger Conant and John Woodbury sureties, 1630/31, for his appearance for death of Thomas Puckett.

FAUNCE, John. *Anne,* 1623.

FELLS, Capt. John, commissioned to carry passengers and goods to Va., May, 1623; granted land there before June, 1623; master of ship *Jacob,* 80 tons, 1623; shipwrecked on Cape Cod December, 1626; wintered at Plymouth, N. E., 1626–27; in Boston Harbor spring of 1627; to Va. fall of 1627.

FENTON, Thomas, agreed, 22 October, 1622, to go to N. E. as calker. (Council for N. E.)

FISBELL, Thomas, agreed, 22 October, 1622, to go to N. E. as calker. (Council for N. E.)

FITCHER, Lieut., Mt. Wollaston, 1625.

FLAVEL, Thomas. *Fortune,* 1621.

FORD, Martha. *Fortune,* 1621.

FROST, ——, 3 *s.* due Frost for "lether" on account of Morton's arrest, 1628; if Nicholas, he was for theft from Indians at Damerills Cove, 1632, etc., fined, whipped, branded in hand with hot iron and banished; if ever found in Massachusetts to be put to death.

FULLER, Edward. *Mayflower,* 1620.

FULLER, Dr. Samuel. *Mayflower,* 1620.

GARDNER, Mr. Thomas, in charge of planting at Cape Ann, 1624; Naumkeag, 1626; 2nd wife, Damaris Shattuck, a Quaker. Born about 1592; died in the winter of 1675/6.

GARLAND, Peter, swore in 1640 he had known Casco River and "frequented the place for 14 years"; Charlestown, 1637; Boston, 1654. Trelawny Papers, p. 239.

GIBBONS, Major Edward, "with Morton of Merrymont before the settlement of Boston" (Lechford, p. 238, note); Salem, 1629; at Charlestown, 1629; fined for abusing himself disorderly with drinking too much strong drink at Mr. Maverick's house at Winnisimmet, 1631; Capt. Artillery Co., 1641; Major General, 1649; died 1654. Joshua Scottowe said that he was "no Debauchee but of a Jocund Temper, and one of the Merry Mounts Society who chose to Dance about a *May pole* — than to hear a good Sermon."

GIBBONS, William, familiar with Casco Bay for 17 years in 1640; one of Levett's 10 men left at House Island, 1624. (Trelawny, p. 231.)

GODBERTSON, Godbert. *Anne,* 1623.

?GODFREY, Mr. Edward, in Maine, 1609? ("a promoter of N. E. 45 years" in 1654); backer of New Plymouth, 1620; at Wessagusset? 1622 ("32 years an adventurer for settling N. E."); attorney for Mason and Georges, 1629–30; had under him 6 great shallops, 5 fishing boats, 13 skiffs; York, 1630; see Provincial Papers, N. H., p. 68. Mayor Gorgeana (York), 1642; Gov. Province of Maine, 1649; died about 1667. Widow Anne; dau. Alice mar. Nicholas Shapleigh. Pope's Pioneers, p. 80. Col. Banks says that Godfrey was financially interested in Maine in the years mentioned above, but that there is no evidence that he came over before 1629.

GORGES, Capt. Robert, Gent., Lieut. Gen. and Gov. of N. E.;
Wessagusset, 1623; at Little Harbor (Piscataqua) spring,
1624; to England, 1624, and died 1628.

GRAY, John, Natascot (Hull), 1622; sold house in Lynn, 1639.

GRAY, Thomas, received Natascot, 1622, from Chikatawbut, sagamore of the Massachusetts Indians; Cape Ann, 1625; Naumkeag, 1626; Marble Harbor (Marblehead), 1631. Living
1660. If the same person, he was banished 1630, and Winthrop, 1632, was blamed by T. Dudley for not enforcing the
decree. October, 1631, his house at Marble Harbor to be
pulled down and "no Englishman shall hereafter give house-
room to him or entertain him." In 1638 to be whipped and
banished. In 1639 Warriner fined for "excessive drinking
at Thom: Grayes at Marble Heade." In 1639 whipped and
fined for being drunk, profaning the name of God, keeping
a tippling house and drawing a knife. In 1640 whipped.
Some say this was persecution. See *Boston Transcript*, 2 June,
1909.

?GREAR, John. "May have come with Mr. Thomson" (Libby,
p. 9); mentioned early as on the Piscataqua; possibly an Indian. See Peach.

GREENE, Mr. Richard, Wessagusset, 1622; brother-in-law of
Thomas Weston; died at Plymouth autumn 1622.

HAMPDEN, Mr. John, met by Phinehas Pratt on the run from
Wessagusset, 1623, with "Mr. Hamdin, I am Glad to see
you alive." The conversation is in Mass. His. Soc. Coll.,
ser. 4, vol. 4, p. 484. Young says he came "in the *Charity*
which brought Weston's colony." Probably in the *Sparrow*
with Pratt since Pratt knew him. The famous Hampden
perhaps. "His identity 'favored by many circumstances.'"
Goodwin, p. 257. "Master John Hamden (a gentleman of
London who then wintered with us and desired much to see
the country.") — *E. Winslow*.

HANSON, Captain, sent from Wessagusset by Robert Gorges in
1623 to seize Thomas Weston at Plymouth. Bradford refused to honor the warrant. Perhaps the Captain was related to Alice Hanson, Bradford's mother, and Gorges hoped
it would influence the Governor.

HATHERLEY, Mr. Timothy. *Anne*, 1623.

HEALE, Dr. Giles, admitted to freedom of Guild of Barber Surgeons, London, 3 August, 1619; came in *Mayflower*, 1620; witnessed will of William Mullins; returned to London, April, 1621; in practice Drury Lane, parish of St. Giles in the Field, until death; buried 3 February, 1652/3. Not mentioned by Bradford. See Banks, M. H. S. Proc., February, 1927.

HICKS, Robert. *Fortune*, 1621.

?HIGGINS, Richard, boy with Edward Wynne at Newfoundland, 1622; if same one, Plymouth, 1623, or perhaps Salem, 1629; Plymouth, 1633; Eastham, Mass.; New Piscataqua, N. J., 1669; dead in 1677; widow Mary and children.

?HILTON, Mr. Edward, apprenticed 1611 to Marie, widow of Charles Hilton of Fishmonger's Company, London. His life, 1621–28, not known; Dover, N. H., or Hilton's Point; died 1671. Some say he did not come over from London until late.

HILTON, Mr. William, of Northwich, Co. Chester, and London; brother of Edward; *Fortune* to Plymouth, 1621; his wife and two children in the *Anne*, 1623; in "a little tyme following" their arrival they went to Piscataqua (1624 or later); Dover; Kittery, part now Eliot, 1634. In sympathy with Rev. John Lyford. Died York, Maine, 1655 or 1656. For a charming letter to the younger Gov. Winthrop see Mass. Hist. Soc. Proc., November, 1895, p. 361. Had children William and Mary.

HILTON, William, Jr. Bapt. Witton church, Northwich, 22 June, 1617; came in *Anne*, 1623, to Plymouth; in Piscataqua, 1623 or 1624; of Newbury and Charlestown; died 7:7:1675. N. E. Hist. Gen. Reg., January, 1882. He had a brother, also William, of York.

HOLMAN, Edward. *Anne*, 1623.

HOPKINS, Mr. Stephen. *Mayflower*, 1620.

?HOSKINS, Nicholas, b. 1589; in Va. 1616; wife came 1620; with Capt. Edward Wynne at Ferriland, Avalon, Newfoundland, 1622; living with child Margaret in Va., 1623–4; of Accomack, Va., 1626; schoolteacher, Portsmouth, 1660; "goodman Hoskins" there in 1676. Va. Hist. Mag., II, 80. *May be several men with the same name.*

?HOWELL, Morgan, "came with Vines," says the historian of
Saco. (Vines came several times, 1609 to 1633.) Cape Porpoise, Maine (Arundel, Kennebunkport). Howell died bet.
1666 and 1667.

HOWLAND, John. *Mayflower,* 1620.

JEFFREYS, William, Gent., "an old planter," Wessagusset, 1623;
Naumkeag, 1626; with Gorges, Bursley, *et al.,* had grant on
east side of Agamenticus River, 2 December, 1631; Freeman, 1631; Jeffreys Creek (Manchester); Newport, R. I.,
1655. Called "my very good gossip," 1634, by Morton.
Died 2 January, 1675, at Newport, aged 84. Will mentions
mother Audry, who was Audry Harvey, wife of William
Jeffray of Chittingly Co., Sussex, and niece of William Harvey, famous Clarenceux King of Arms and Antiquary. See
Visitation. He had a brother and 7 sisters of whom 5 were
wives of London merchants.

JENNEY, John. *Little James,* 1623.

JOHNSON, Edward, Gent., merchant, born about 1593–97; perhaps of a prominent seafaring family of Stepney, Middlesex;
judge in the case of stealing at Wessagusset, 1622; desired
to be a freeman, 1630; licensed trader on Merrimac River,
1631–32; north side of Piscataqua, 1636; mayor of Gorgeana?; oath of allegiance to Mass., 1652; province com. 1667;
in 1676 he stated he had been 55 years in the country (Col.
Banks); age 89 in 1682; killed in York Massacre, 1692?
Executor mentioned in will, 1631, of James Damerill of
Stepney, England, who died "overseas."

?JOHNSON, Francis, Gent., with Conant, Palfrey and Dix in
trading Co., 1631; Marblehead, 1644; born 1604; died 1691.
See also N. E. Hist. Gen. Register, vol. 13, p. 170.

KEMPTON, Manasseh. *Anne,* 1623.

KEY, William, agreed, 22 October, 1622, to go to N. E. as calker.
(Council for N. E.)

KNIGHT, Walter, born 1587; Natascot, 1622; Cape Ann, 1625;
Naumkeag, 1626; living in Boston 1653. Not a member of
the Salem church. Fined, 1640, for rude speeches. Lived
with his wife before marriage but not so much after marriage.

?LANE, Thomas, in 1634 "late servant to John Burslyn, fallen lame and impotent." Dorchester, 1634; inhab. of Wessagusset, to be charged for his support.

LATHAM, William. *Mayflower,* 1620.

"LEAVER, Master," came in *Mayflower,* 1620; Mourt's Relation, 12 January, 1620/21, says he with others went to rescue two persons lost. Col. Banks accepts the name. Goodwin and Arber call him Carver.

LESTER, Edward. *Mayflower,* 1620.

LEVETT, Capt. Christopher, Isles of Shoals, November, 1623; Little Harbor (also called Pannaway) spring 1624; Casco, 1624, and returned 1624 to England; in Royal Navy until 1628; in N. E. June, 1630; died at sea. James Savage in Winthrop's History thinks Levett at Salem, 1630, a different man.

LEWIS, Thomas, Gent., patent, 1629, of land between Cape Elizabeth and Cape Porpoise. His name associated with "old planters," Blaxton, Jeffreys, Hilton, and with Bonython. In the patent dated 12 February, 1629–30, with R. Bonython he says he had "already been at the charge to transport himself and others to Take a view of New England." (Banks.) Oath of allegiance November, 1652. His dau. Mary mar. Rev. Richard Gibson about 1638, an Episcopalian. Mary was a troublesome person. Gibson wrote to Winthrop in 1638: "She so behaved her self in the shipp which brought her from England hither some two years agoe that the block was reaved at the Mayne yard to have duckt her."

LONG, Robert. *Anne,* 1623.

LYFORD, Rev. John, B.A., Magdalen College, Oxford, 1597; Prebendary of Loughall, Ireland, 1613; Coventry (?), Warwick, 1615; came with wife Sarah and several children; March, 1623–4, in *Charity,* perhaps with E. Winslow; New Plymouth, 1624, where he preached; Natascot, 1624; Cape Ann, 1625; Naumkeag, 1626–27; Minister of Martin's Hundred, Virginia, 1629; his will, dated 9 February, 1629/30, was proved 19 May, 1632; in Va. 1631 when son Obadiah matriculated; he had held lease of lands at Levalaglesh, Manor of Dromully, Co. Armagh, Ireland, and free lands in Ocorigan, County Tyrone. His children were Mordecai, Rev. Obadiah, Ruth, Anne, and perhaps Martha, wife of Samuel Lincoln, and ancestress of Abraham Lincoln (N. Y. G. and B. Record, April, 1929). His widow Sarah married Edmund Hobart of Hingham 10 October, 1634, and died in 1639, aged 53. (See Lechford, page 93.)

?LYNN, Henry, Boston; punished September, 1630; banished 1631 for slander against govt. and churches; banishment remitted; here in 1636; York, 1645; Virginia, where he died. (See also Pickering.)

MARTIN, Mr. Christopher. *Mayflower,* 1620.

MAVERICK, Mr. Samuel, born 1602, son of Rev. John Maverick of Devon; Wessagusset, 1623; Winnesimmet, 1625; possibly agent for Levett, 1627; about 1628 married Amias, widow of David Thomson; Noddles Island, 1634; visited there 1638 by John Josselyn; about 1660 wrote a Description of N. E.; N. Y., 1664 (King's Commissioner); died there bet. 1670 and 1676. See N. E. Hist. Gen. Reg., April, 1915. Also Maine Province Court Record, vol. 1, p. xlvii.

MILLS, John, testified 1640 he had known Casco River 13 or 14 years (1626–7); Richmond Island, 1633; of Black Point (Scarborough); died 1675.

MITCHELL, Experience. *Anne,* 1623.

MORE, Richard. *Mayflower,* 1620.

MORGAN, Benedict. *Fortune,* 1621.

MORRELL, Rev. William, B.A., Magdalene College, Cambridge, 1614–15; ordained 1619; Wessagusset, 1623; Plymouth, winter 1624–5; sailed for England spring 1625. In 1625 published a long poem in Latin and English descriptive of New England.

MORTON, George. *Little James,* 1623.

MORTON, Thomas, of Clifford's Inn, London, Gent., married, 1621, Alice Miller, widow; said he came 1622 to Wessagusset but probably an error; Mt. Wollaston (Quincy), 1625, with 30 servants; arrested 1628 at Mt. Wollaston (Merrymount) and sent to England; back to N. E. 1629; imprisoned

1630 and sent to England; returned to N. E.; "in N. E. nine or ten years," 1634; "being of late enforced from those forraigne parts by the mallitious practice of the separatists there that have seized and taken away all the meanes that your subject was possessed of in those parts," 1636; in 1644 fined £100; died at Agamenticus (York) 1646 "poor and despised." Author of "New English Canaan."

MORTON, Thomas, Jr. *Anne*, 1623.

MULLINS, Mr. William. *Mayflower*, 1620.

NEWTON, Ellen. *Anne*, 1623.

?NODDLE, William, of Noddle's Island, Boston Harbor; island so called 24 December, 1630, by Winthrop although Noddle apparently no longer there; freeman, 18 May, 1631; Salem, 1632; drowned from canoe, South River, June, 1632. A Lincolnshire name. May have come with Endecott 1628 or Higginson 1629, but I "feel" that he was here earlier. Conant's Island and Thompson's Island in the Bay were both named for men here before 1628.

NORMAN, John, Cape Ann, 1624, aged 11. Naumkeag, 1626; Manchester, 1640; Marblehead, 1648; died 1672. Said to have lived near the spot where later the *Hesperus* was wrecked.

NORMAN, Richard (old goodman), Cape Ann, 1624; Naumkeag, 1626; Marblehead, 1650. In 1674 Richard of Marblehead, aged 50, deposed. (Reg., April, 1896, p. 202.)

OLDHAM, Mr. John, perhaps from Derby, England; came in *Anne* 1623 with wife, sister, and seven associates; his sister Lucretia married, 1624, Jonathan Brewster (whose older brother had returned to the Established church) and son of Elder William Brewster; Natascot, 1624; refused to go to Cape Ann in charge of trading with the Indians 1624; to England in charge of T. Morton, 1628; returned to N. E. 1629; delegate to court from Watertown; patentee with Vines, 1630; in August, 1632, his "small house near the wear at Watertown made all of clapboards, burnt down"; killed 1636, having with him John Oldham aged 13 and Thomas aged 11. "Less disposed to overlook this world, in his re-

gard for the next, than most of his early neighbors."—*Savage.*
See also William Bridge. The seven who came with Oldham
were perhaps dau. Mary, one Richard Oldham (of Cambridge), and friends.

PALFREY, Peter, Naumkeag, 1626; Reading (Wakefield), 1652;
town officer both places; died 1663.

PALMER, William. *Fortune, 1621.*

PARKER, John, mate of the *Mayflower,* 1620; spent the winter at
Plymouth, 1620–21; at Monhegan 1629 and perhaps much
earlier; Saco, 1636; died before June, 1661; uncle of
Col. John Phillips of Charlestown; owned Parker's Island
(Georgetown), Maine. See M. H. S. Proc., April, 1927,
p. 216. Also Mass. Sup. Jud. Ct. Files, paper 2164. Children, Thomas, John, Mary.

PASCO, ——, Isles of Shoals?; Gibbons paid him for shirt at Morton's arrest, 1628.

?PATCH (Edmund?), Wessagusset 1622(?); Naumkeag 1626(?);
proprietor Salem 1639; died 1680. Butler's Hudibras (Part
II, canto II, lines 409-440) speaks of the case where a
cobbler at Wessagusset stole corn or killed a red man, and an
invalid weaver was said to have been executed in his stead
to appease the Indians.

"The mighty Tottipottymoy
complaining sorely of the breach
of league, held forth by brother Patch."

C. F. Adams says (Three Episodes, vol. I, p. 81), that
Butler may have heard the story with details from Thomas
Morton who mentions the incident in his *New English
Canaan* but without the man's name. If Patch is an imag-
inary name why did not the poet select one to rhyme with
"breach"? Felt says "a Patch family was in Salem as early
as 1629." This may be Edmund Patch, baptized 1601;
Salem, 1639; died 1680. See N. E. Hist. Gen. Reg., April,
1917.

Arthur Peach was executed in 1638 for killing an Indian.
If Butler fused the two stories there may have been no early
colonist named Patch, the name being used to conceal the
obvious rhyme.

PEACH, ——, called "old father Peach" in 1633 in a letter of
John Raymond to Mr. Ambrose Gibbons at Newichawannock. (Provincial Papers, New Hampshire, Bouton, vol. 1,
page 76.) From an enlarged photostat of the letter sent me
by Mr. Otis G. Hammond the following reading has been
agreed upon by Mr. Albert Matthews, Miss Wildman and
Miss Gregory, who have studied the handwriting with me:
"Mr. Gibbons. You shall rec(eive) by the bearer Grear
John three bundles of lace with six bundles of taipe wch I
pray rec. for ould father peach who owes me 2 lb 3 ounces
of beaver whereof I pray take notice of."
John Peach Senior of Salem (born 1614) and his brother
John Peach Junior of Marblehead (born 1616) may have
been his sons. Mr. Libby (page 9) groups old Father Peach
with others who "may have come with Mr. Thomson."

PEDDOCK, Leonard, a London merchant; lic. to marry Elizabeth
Wynston of Plymouth, widow, 3 December, 1618; 8 November, 1622, to receive £10 "for his last employments" in New
England (State Papers, Colon., 1574–1660, p. 34); order to
carry "Unipa Whinett" over 19 November, 1622; of St.
Catherine Colman parish, London, when his dau. Hannah
was bapt. 7 September, 1623. (Col. Banks.)

PENN, Christian. *Anne,* 1623.

?PICKERING, John, "may have come with Mr. Thomson" (Libby,
p. 9). "Portsmouth perhaps as early as 1630" (*Savage*);
possibly the John Pickryn to sit in stocks at Salem 1630 with
Henry Lynn and John Boggust, accessory to felony by John
Goulworth; in Capt. Neale's cash account after 1633; gave
bonds 1635 for Nicholas Frost; in Piscataqua court 1642;
deposed in 1660, aged about 60; died 1668 or 1669. See
Pope, p. 163.

PIDDOCK, Thomas, in June-July, 1624, at Monhegan as factor
for Jennings and Cross, Plymouth merchants (Libby's Gen.
Dict., p. 2); of London, 1628, aged 27.

POMFRET, William, distiller, offers 30 November, 1622, to go to
N. E. (Council for N. E.); factor for Jennings and Cross
at Monhegan June-July, 1624 (Libby's Gen. Dict., p. 2);
Dover, N. H., 1640; town clerk, etc., 1648; died 7 August,
1680.

PRATT, Joshua. *Anne*, 1623.

PRATT, Phinehas, Wessagusset, 1622; at Little Harbor (Piscataqua) May, 1623; moved to Plymouth; Charlestown, 1677; died there 19 April, 1680. Biog. in *Mayflower Desc.*, vol. IV.

PRENCE, Mr. Thomas. *Fortune*, 1621.

PRIEST, Degory. *Mayflower*, 1620.

PURCHASE, Mr. Thomas, came "neare three scoore years since" (1684); Maine, 1624; on Stevens or New Meadows River, Pejepscot (Brunswick), between 1624 and 1628; married, 1631, Mary Grove, Sir Christopher Gardiner's lady friend about whom so much fiction and poetry have been written (M. H. S. Proc., January, 1883, pp. 79, 87); Magistrate of Merrymeeting Bay district 1654; she died 1655–6; married (2) Elizabeth Williams, and had five children; he died May 11, 1677, aged 101. York Deeds, Book 4. Wheeler's Brunswick, p. 788.

RASTELL, Mr. Humphrey, at Cape Ann aboard the *Unity* 1624; at Mt. Wollaston 1625; London and Virginia merchant. "A collerick and hott" merchant, much with Capt. Wollaston; owner ship *Anne*, 1628. Died in Virginia before end of October, 1628; heir was Thomas Rastell of London. See Minutes Council of Va.

RATLIFFE, Robert. *Anne*, 1623.

RICHARD (Thomas?), had 18s. from Gibbons at time of Morton's arrest, 1628.

?RICHMOND, George, of Bandon Bridge, Ireland, a merchant with ship and men; Richmond Island probably named for him. See Baxter's "George Cleeve," pp. 19, 20. Mr. John Richmond's servant detained by Mr. Thomas Lewis 1636/7.

ROBERTS, Thomas, at Dover (Winachahanat) spring of 1623(?) with the Hiltons; had been a fishmonger in London; will probated 30 June, 1674. Several children. Provincial Papers, N. H., vol. 1, p. 118; A. H. Quint's Hist. Mem., pp. 91, 176.

ROGERS, Rev. Mr., brought over to Plymouth spring of 1628 by Isaac Allerton; a young man "crased in his braine"; sent back in 1629. (Bradford II, 58.)

If the "Rev Mr Rogers" of Bradford's *History* was the same as "Mr Bubble" of *The New English Canaan* we learn from a marginal note in the latter work that his Christian name was John, and hence perhaps admitted to Clare College 1616, B.A. 1620–21, M.A. 1624, ordained 1625–26. Morton says that Mr Bubble was "Master of Ceremonies" and "house chaplain" at Plymouth when Oldham was absent, namely in the winter of 1628–29. Rogers was minister there at that period. Morton says that Mr Bubble was "mazed," and tells a story of a trip to the Nipmuck country for beaver skins which proves it. Bradford says that Rogers was "crased in his braine." Morton says that Mr Bubble was a scholar interested in the Indian language. If Bubble is Rogers this interest would explain why Isaac Allerton brought Rogers over at the Company's expense in the spring of 1628.

Mr Bubble was a big-boned man, a scholar, acquainted with shorthand, a poor sportsman, a dull preacher, and fond of long prayers. It is not strange that Mr Bubble disgusted Morton and Mr Rogers displeased Bradford.

Rogers, Thomas. *Mayflower,* 1620.

?Rouse, Nicholas, at Levett's house at Casco 1630; from Wembery, Devon. Wessagusset, 1622? Four of Weston's 1622 party at Casco 1627. Trelawny Papers, Maine Hist. Soc. Coll., 2nd ser., vol. 3, p. 251.

Salisbury, Dr., Wessagusset, 1623.

Sampson, Henry. *Mayflower,* 1620.

Sanders, John, Wessagusset, 1622; "overseer" after Greene died 1622; to Monhegan February, 1622/23; did not return.

Shapleigh, Alexander, "came to the Piscataqua Valley at a very early day," Strawberry Bank and Kittery.

Shaw, John, Wessagusset, 1623?; in division of cattle Plymouth, 1627; "John Shaw Sr" of Weymouth 1672/3; 9 September, 1704, "dyed old goodman Shaw of Weymouth pretty suddenly." Goodwin, Pilgrim Republic, p. 297, says that Shaw and Phinehas Pratt of the division did not come in any Pilgrim ship. Closely associated in land sales (*Mayflower Desc.,* vol. 4, 1902, p. 96). Of course Shaw may have come in a fishing ship, not with Pratt.

SHURT, Mr. Abraham, at Pemaquid 1626 (July 24) where he acknowledged a deed; trader on coast 1643; dead before 1647?

SIBSIE, Capt. John, shipwrecked on Cape Cod December, 1626; wintered Plymouth, N. E., 1626–7; fined at James City, Va., for not attending church 1629; Council Va., 1637; house of Burgesses, 1632–41; died 1652. Lived in Princess Anne County.

SIMONSON, Moses. *Fortune*, 1621.

SMALEY (Elizabeth), widow of Capt. Robert, transient in New England, 1624. Gov. Wyatt of Va. wrote 2 December, 1624, "Widow Smaley when she arrives from New England shall find all lawful favour." (Colon. Papers, p. 70.) She married Randall Crew of Virginia as her second husband.

SNOW, Nicholas. *Anne*, 1623.

SOULE, George. *Mayflower*, 1620.

SOUTHWORTH, Alice. *Anne*, 1623.

SPRAGUE, Francis. *Anne*, 1623.

STEVENS, Thomas, at Pejepscot (Brunswick) "not long after 1624" on Stevens's or New Meadows River; (see Reg., October, 1867, p. 357); house burnt 1676; in 1688 he was captured by Indians (deposition Me. Hist. Soc. Coll. Doc. Hist., ser. 2, vol. 6, p. 421) but his age is wrong; widow Margaret lived on Swan Island.

STACIE, Hugh. *Fortune*, 1621.

STANDISH, Capt. Myles. *Mayflower*, 1620.

?STONE, Capt. John, a stormy sea captain, fined for confronting authority 1633; murdered January, 1633/4; Ford suggests that he was of the Wessagusset Colony. (Mass. Hist. Soc. Proc., January, 1918, p. 230.)

?SWADDON, Philip, whipped for running away, 1631; free from his master, Robert Seeley of Watertown, 1631; wigwam at Piscataqua, 1636; Strawberry Bank, 1640; living 1673, aged 73. Could he be Swabber of John Pory's letter 1622? See also Libby's Dict., p. 9.

TAYLOR, John, of "Jalme" (Yealm?) Devon, boat master for Winter at Casco Bay 1627.

TENCH, William. *Fortune*, 1621.

THOMSON, Mr. David, merchant Plymouth, England; mar., 1613, Amias Cole; agent for Council for N. E.; in N. E. 1623, perhaps came in *Jonathan of Plymouth;* Piscataqua, April-May, 1623; Plymouth, summer 1623; Piscataqua, 1623–26; Thomson's Island, 1626; died 1627 or 1628. Widow who spoke of her fatherless children married about 1628 Samuel Maverick. A son, John Thomson, was living in 1650.

TILDEN, Thomas. *Anne*, 1623.

TILLEY, John. *Mayflower*, 1620.

TRACY, Stephen. *Anne*, 1623.

TRASK, Capt. William, Naumkeag, 1626; in Pequot War 1637; died 1666. Ensign and color bearer when Capt. Endecott cut the cross of St. George from the flag. In protest he named his next daughter Truecross Trask.

TREVORE, William, seaman hired with Ellis or Ely to come in the *Mayflower* and stay a year; on the coast with Dermer in 1619 if his deposition is to be believed; with Standish in the Bay September, 1621, when Thompson's Island was seen and called Island Trevore; master of *Handmaid*, 1628, which carried Morton to England; master of *William* December, 1632, and touched at New Plymouth. Died after 7 May, 1650.

TUCKER, Mr. Richard, Spurwink, 1627; died 1679.

TURNER, John. *Mayflower*, 1620.

TYLLY, Mr. John, overseer of fishing Cape Ann 1624; "now resident at Cape Ann" 1625; Naumkeag, 1626; trading voyage to Conn. River 1636; captured, hands and feet cut off, died 1636. "Very stout (courageous?) man and of great understanding. . . . He cried not in his torture."—*Winthrop*.

VENGHAM, William, "planted upon that island (Monhegan)" June-July, 1624. "A man of experience in those parts"— Damariscove (Putnam's Gen. Mag., December, 1916). William "Venyham" mar. at Plymouth, 1616, Agnes Dibb.

VINES, Dr. Richard, Winter Harbor, 1616–17; patent 1629; governor of the plantation of Saco 1639; chosen deputy governor Province of Maine 21 October, 1645; "to Barbadoes 1645 and a physician there" until his burial 19 April, 1651. An Episcopalian. He lived in St. Michael's Parish and grew cotton, tobacco and sugar. His will mentions daughters Margaret (Mrs. Thomas Ellicott), Joan (Mrs. Ducy), Elizabeth, and a granddaughter, Belinda Parrasite, under 15 in 1651. (Reg. April, 1900.)

WALFORD, Thomas, Wessagusset, 1623; Mishawum (Charlestown), 1625; banished 1631; Portsmouth, 1631; grand jury 1650; church warden 1640; died 1667. He signed a deed in 1648 by a mark and his will in 1666 in the same manner. See Stackpole's Hist. N. H., vol. 1, p. 22.

WALLEN, Ralph. *Anne*, 1623.

WARREN, Mr. Richard. *Mayflower*, 1620.

?WAY, George, at Pejepscot with brother-in-law Thomas Purchase "not long after 1624," near head of New Meadows River. (Reg., October, 1867, p. 357. See will in Reg., April, 1889, p. 151.) Died Dorchester, England, October, 1641. Had son Eleazer at Hartford, Conn. Wheeler's Brunswick, p. 10, doubts his being here.

WESTON, Andrew, London ironmonger; came 1622 to Wessagusset; returned in *Charity* autumn of 1622; brother of Thomas Weston. See Mass. Hist. Soc. Proc., January, 1921, p. 165. (Banks.)

WESTON, Mr. Thomas, of St. Giles in the Fields, London, merchant, financed the Pilgrims 1620; Wessagusset, 1622; cast away at Hampton or Rye (south of Piscataqua) June-July, 1623; too humane to traffic in indentured servants for Virginia, 1624–5; Maryland, 1642; in assembly 1642; had Westbury manor there; to England, 1644–5; died 1645–47. His dau. Elizabeth mar. Roger Conant, Jr., and had a son John. See N. E. H. Gen. Reg., April, 1896, p. 209 (Johnston).

WHITE, Rowland, and his boy, agreed 22 October, 1622, to go to N. E. as calkers. (Council for N. E.)

WHITE, Mr. William. *Mayflower,* 1620.

WILLS, Bennett, of Plymouth, boatswain for Winter at Casco Bay 1627.

WINSLOW, Mr. Edward. *Mayflower,* 1620.

WINSLOW, John. *Fortune,* 1621.

WINTER, John, "At Casko that yeare that I did fish which is about som 13 yeares past" (i. e., 1627); agent for Trelawny and Goodyear December 1, 1631, when he was at Richmond Island; d. 1648. An able, wise manager of a fishing station.

WOLLASTON, Captain, with Raleigh at Guiana 1617; at Cape Ann aboard the *Unity* 1624; in Va. October, 1624; Mt. Wollaston, 1625; before General Court 1641 (?).

WOODBURY, Humphrey, came with father John in June, 1628, to Naumkeag. Testified in 1680 about his father's migration.

WOODBURY, John, Cape Ann, 1624; Naumkeag, 1626; in England 1628; Bass River (Beverly) 1630 with brother William; died 1641.

WRIGHT, William. *Fortune,* 1621.

## APPENDIX B

# EARLY SETTLEMENTS AND THEIR FOUNDERS

### CAPE ANN (near GLOUCESTER)

1623–4    14 settlers in 1624          William Allen
Never above 50.            Roger Conant
See Naumkeag.           Thomas Gardner

1624      Plymouth Colony and the Dor-   Thomas Gray
chester adventurers each had a fish-  Walter Knight
ing stage at Cape Ann.        Rev. John Lyford
Levett said the harbor was good   John Norman
but too far from the fishing    Richard Norman
grounds, and fertile soil limited.   John Tylly
                                          John Woodbury

1624      Minutes Council of Va.:—

Cap$^t$ *Marten* beeing att *Cape Ane* aboard in the good ship called the *Vnity;* Cap$^t$ *Woolaston* and M$^r$. *Rastell* coming aboard the same ship, falling in to conference about their affayres, M$^r$. *Rastell* the M$^r$chant grew collerick and hott, beeing demanded of Cap$^t$ *Marten* wherfore hee kept prisoner in that kind, and would make noe dispatch for *Virginia.*

### CASCO, LEVETT'S PALISADED HOUSE at, 1624

(On House Island between South Portland and Peak Island.) Jenness says that the peninsula of Portland was called Quack or York.

1623–4    Ten men were left there in 1624   Christopher Levett
when Levett went back to England   William Gibbons

1624      4 men of Weston's colony there in   Thomas Alger
1624; perhaps also in 1623. Win-  ?John Badiver
ter hired them at Casco in 1630.   Edmund Baker
"C. Levett" (Baxter), p. 126.     Nicholas Rouse

1627     John Winter wrote in 1640:       John Winter

"4 ships did fysh at Casko that     Ambrose Bauden[2]
yeare that I did fish which is about   John Tayler[3]
som 13 yeares past." Trelawny,     Bennett Wills[4]
p. 250. Year 1640.                   ?John Cousins[1]
[1] There in 1626.                    ?Peter Garland[1]
[2] Of Holberton, Devon, Winter's    ?John Mills[1]
apprentice.
[3] Of Jalme (Yealm?) Devon, mariner, "a bootes master when I did
fish at Casko."
[4] Of Plymouth, a "boteson" and
"bootes master."
In November, 1627, Levett said he
must order his servants to come
away if his plans were not accepted
in London.

## DAMARISCOVE (off CAPE NEWAGEN and BOOTHBAY HARBOR)

("Damerils Iles" in Smith's time, 1614; "I. Damar Elscove,"
1647.) In 1780 drawn as two islands. Still so in extreme high
tide.

1614     "Damerils Iles"               Captain [James?]
1622     About which place ["Damarin's     Damerill
Cove] there fished above thirty    Humphrey Damerill
sail of ships. (Good newes from    William Vengham
N. E.)                         —— Corbin[1]
1622–26 A plantation at Damrills Cove,    Jeffrey Cornish[2]
"Canada."                    ?William Edwards
John Pory in 1622 found 13 men
and 10 dogs.
See Libby's Gen. Dict., p. 2. Also
Min. of Council of Va.

1622    When the *Sparrow* arrived in May Phinehas Pratt wrote: "Wanting a pilote we Arived att Damoralls Cove. The men y^t belong to y^e ship, ther fishing, had newly set up a may pole & weare very mery. We maed hast to prepare a boat fit for costing."
[1] "One Corbin of Canada" offered fish to Luke Edan 1624. There was a Capt. John Corbin 1633. Robert was of Casco in 1658.
[2] In 1625 "at Dambrells Cove Jefferey Cornish came abourd the ship caled ye *Swan*."

1631    About 15 fishing boats there after 1631. (Davis.)


## ELIZABETH'S ISLE (CUTTYHUNK)

1602    34 persons.
Here in May, and June, 1602, on the "Concord."
[1] In 1605 with Weymouth.
[2] In 1603 with Pring.
Cuttyhunk means cultivated or broken ground (W. B. Cabot).

Bartholomew Gosnold
Bartholomew Gilbert
Gabriel Archer
James Rosier[1]
John Brereton
Robert Salterne[2]
John Angel
William Street
John Tucker


## ISLES OF SHOALS
### (Smith Isles, 1614)

1622    Pratt says the *Sparrow's* shallop touched here in 1622. He was back the next spring to fish.

1623 (spring)    Levett wrote: "Upon these islands I neither could see one good timber tree, nor so much ground as to make a garden.

"The place is found to be a good fishing place for six ships, but more cannot well be there, for want of convenient stage room, as this year's experience hath proved.

"The harbor is but indifferent good. Upon these islands are no savages at all."

1628 Perhaps at Isles of Shoals Morton was marooned in 1628 for a month without "gunne, powther, or shot or dogge or so much as a knife." Bradford, II., 57. New English Canaan, pages 144, 151. Morton complained of his thin suit of clothes, and in the account of expenditure in which these names appear a suit of clothes was purchased. They may not have been at the Islands for Morton suggests that Indians only were with him there. [1] Thomas Richard was servant to Edward Astley at the Penobscot, and dead in 1631.

[Benjamin?] Cribbe
[Nicholas?] Frost
—— Pasco
[Thomas?] Richard[1]

1630 Winthrop saw "a ship lie there at anchor, and five or six shallops under sail up and down."

1852 Nathaniel Hawthorne spent six weeks on Appledore Island. His American Note-Books record impressions of a trained observer. Conditions changed very little in two centuries. He speaks of hearing the surf at Odiorne's Point (Little Harbor).

## MISHAWUM (CHARLESTOWN)

1625 Man and wife.
In 1630 Roger Clap found "some wigwams and one house. In the

Thomas Walford

house there was a man which had
a boiled bass, but no bread that we
see." Walford, "an old planter,"
gave Clap's party the bass and
asked the Indians not to come
near them in the night.

1628–9    "First inhabitants"                     The Spragues and
          Young's Chronicles (1846), p. 375.      half a dozen others


## MT. WOLLASTON, PASONAGESSET, or MERRYMOUNT (QUINCY)
### (Two miles north of Wessagusset)

1625–28   Three or four gentlemen and some       Walter Bagnall
          "30 servants," or men who had sold     Lieut. Fitcher
          their time.                            Edward Gibbons
          The adventure is described in Mor-     Thomas Morton
          ton's New English Canaan.              Humphrey Rastell
1626      Wollaston took all but six to          Capt. Wollaston
          Virginia.
1627.     A Maypole erected, a custom ob-
          served at Damariscove and else-
          where. The New English Canaan,
          book 3, chapter 14, gives no indica-
          tion of improper revels.
          Objection was made to the sale of
          guns and rum to the Indians. The
          latter was denied by Morton.


## MONHEGAN ISLAND, off PEMAQUID POINT
### (La Nef, 1605; Island St. George, 1610; Barties Island, 1614)

1610      trading post.                          Capt. Williams
1614      (for "many years" before)              Sir Francis Popham's ships
          trading post.
          Smith in May and June took
          40,000 fish.

| | | |
|---|---|---|
| 1618–19 | crew. "Bad lodging and worse fare." | Capt. Edward Rocroft's mutinous crew spent the cold months, preferring it to Winter Harbor, on the Saco. |
| 1622 | owned 1622 by Abraham Jennens of Plymouth. | |
| 1623 | "a scattered beginning." Bradford, who offered to send Weston's people there if they wished to go. | |
| 1624 | Factors for Abraham and Ambrose Jennings and William Cross, Plymouth merchants. | Thomas Piddock, Edmund Dockett, William Pomfret |
| | See C. T. Libby's Gen. Dict., p. 2. | William Vengham "planted there." |
| 1626 | Settlement established by Abraham Shurt, magistrate. | Abraham Shurt |
| 1629 | A fishing post there (Jenney's Monhegan, p. 34). | John Parker |
| 1631 | After 1631 about 31 fishing boats, and 84 farmers here and at Pemaquid (Davis) | |

## NATASCOT (HULL)
### (Then an island)

| | | |
|---|---|---|
| 1622 | "A few fishermen." [1]See Bradford, vol. 1 (1912), p. 418, note. The site probably was Pemberton Landing where water, shelter and anchorage could be had (Fitz Henry Smith). Or possibly further south by the mainland where "Layford's Liking River" (Weir River) running from Straits Pond meets the Bay. | Roger Conant[1] John Gray Thomas Gray Walter Knight Rev. John Lyford John Oldham |

1630    In May, 1630, Roger Clap and
party, set ashore from the *Mary
and John,* got a boat from "some
old planters."

## NAUMKEAG (SALEM)

1626    35 persons, 15 men?                          William Allen
"We found about half a score           John Balch
houses built: and a fayre house        Roger Conant
newly built for the governour."—       Thomas Gardner
Higginson, 1629.  This house was       Thomas Gray
Conant's at Cape Ann, rebuilt.         William Jeffreys
1628    "Only nine men at Salem on the         Walter Knight
arrival of Endicott.  Conant may       Rev. John Lyford
have had his wife and his two sons,    John Norman
Lot and Roger, with him."—W. A.        Richard Norman
Pew.                                   Peter Palfrey
                                       John Tylly
                                       William Trask
                                       John Woodbury

## PEJEPSCOT (BRUNSWICK, MAINE)
### (Stevens River, now New Meadows River)

1628                                       Thomas  Purchase
                                       Thomas Stevens
                                       ? George Way

## PEMAQUID, MAINE
### (Johnstown, 1614)

1614 (before)                              Sir Francis Popham's ships
trading post.
1615–16 crew.                              Sir Richard Hawkins
1622    30 ships trading there-
abouts.
1623    fishing stages.                    Mr. Cox
1625    Maverick in 1660 wrote
of families settled there by
Alderman Aldworth.

| | | |
|---|---|---|
| 1625 | Connected with a deed said by C. T. Libby to be a forgery.<br>[1] Levett in 1623–4 speaks of "Mr. Coke's stage" at Pemaquid. | { ? John Brown<br>{ ? William Cox[1]<br>{ ? Matthew Newman |
| 1626 | Magistrate and local official. | Abraham Shurt |
| 1631 | About 31 fishing boats and 84 farmers here and at Monhegan after 1631 (Davis).<br>Robert Aldworth and Gyles Elbridge of Bristol patentees.<br>Shurt was their agent. | |
| 1632 | Raided by Dixey Bull, pirate, who destroyed the fort. | |

## PENOBSCOT

| | | |
|---|---|---|
| 1628–31 | Trading house.<br>Accused of selling powder and shot to Indians.<br>Among his servants were:<br>John Deacon<br>Henry Sampson<br>George Watson<br>Oliver Callow (in Boston marriage records 1655 given as Callowe)<br>James L——<br>one Muntowes an Indian<br>Thomas Willett<br>Thomas Richard (lately deceased before 19 July, 1631) | Edward Astley and servants |
| 1631 | Matinicus Island in Penobscot Bay had 20 fishing boats after 1631 (Davis). | |

1632 (June)
  Astley to have a license to go to New
  England on furnishing security for
  good behaviour there.

## PISCATAQUA

*Little Harbor* (Odiorne's Point, now in Rye)
Called Pannaway by Levett
(Mouth of River)

| | |
|---|---|
| 1623–24 Trading post; 7 to 10 men. A large stone house called Piscataque House or Capt. Mason's House. Christopher Levett and Robert Gorges here to visit. Edward Godfrey had charge of the fishery later. | David Thomson perhaps with wife ? Edward Hilton |

*Newichawannock* (Dover)
(Hilton's Point, Northam)

| | |
|---|---|
| 1624 or later.   Settlement. Meeting house built 1634 with "entrenchment and flankarts." Thomas Wiggans agent in authority 1631–37; Roberts, 1640. Ambrose Gibbons had charge of the sawmill 1631. | Edward Hilton, wife and children William Hilton, wife and children ? Thomas Roberts and family ? Old Father Peach |

*Strawberry Bank* (Portsmouth)
(Three miles up from the mouth of the River)

1630 ? Walter Neale Governor 1630.
  Thomas Wannerton was at the
  Great House (called rarely Mason's
  Hall) in 1633 under Gorges and
  Mason. Built 1631 by the La-
  conia Co.

1630 "Others hearing of men of their
  own disposition which were planted
  at Pascataway went from us [the
  Winthrop colony] to them." T.
  Dudley's Letter to the Countess.

## PLYMOUTH

1603 Martin Pring there
1620 The *Mayflower,* December     Names of settlers in
                                       Appendix A

### RICHMOND ISLAND
#### (One half mile S. E. of Cape Elizabeth)
#### (Has 200 acres and four coves)

1627 (before)                      ? George Richmond
     Trading post               John Burges
1627 and earlier            Walter Bagnall
     Trading post               John P——[1]
1628–31    "     "           John Winter
1631     See the Trelawny Papers for many   and employees
        names of fishermen.
[1] Possibly John Bray, J. P. Baxter says.
1635     Rev. R. Mather said about 40 per-
        sons were there.
1638     "John Winter a grave and dis-
        creet man . . . imployer of 60
        men."—John Josselyn.

### SAGADAHOC COLONY (POPHAM'S)

1607–8   120 planters in the *Gift of*   Among them were:
       *God* and the *Mary and John.*   George Popham
       See Libby's Geneal. Dict. of   Raleigh Gilbert
       Maine and N. H., p. 2. Also   James Davies
       Mass. Hist. Soc. Proc.,vol. 18.   Rev. Richard Seymour
       Possibly a Captain Damerill   Richard or Robert
       was one.                     Davies
       After 1631 both sides of the   Edward Harlow
       Kennebec had 51 fishing boats   Ellis Best
       (S. Davis).                  —— Digby, shipwright
                                      Master Patteson
                                   —— Leaman, secretary
                                   Gome Carew

#### Col. Banks adds:
Mr. Fosque          Timothy Savage
John Havercombe    John Fletcher
Lancelot Booker      John Elliott?
John Diaman

## SHAWMUT (BOSTON)

1625–35  1 man and servant                    Rev. Wm. Blaxton
Westerly corner Beacon and Spruce
Streets.


## SPURWINK (South shore of CAPE ELIZABETH, MAINE)

(On the mainland between Prouts Neck and Cape Elizabeth.
Richmond Island is off the coast.)

1627      Landowners.                          Richard Tucker
Richard Bradshaw


## THOMPSON'S ISLAND, MASSACHUSETTS BAY

1626      Thomson, wife, son and servants.   David Thomson


## WESSAGUSSET (WEYMOUTH, MASS.)

1622 (Weston) May                           Master's Mate Gibbs
10 in all (Pratt); including 7        and 2 sailors?
passengers from the *Sparrow's*       Phinehas Pratt
pinnace. (Winslow.)                   John Hampden
? John Shaw
and 4 others.


1622 (Weston) June-July                     ? Thomas Alger
60 lusty men in the *Charity* and     ? John Badiver
*Swan*.  A trading adventure.         Edmund Baker
"No chosen Separatists, but men       Richard Greene
made choice of at all adven-          Edward Johnson
tures."—Morton.                       Thomas Morton[1]
[1] "Most of them returned to England."—   ? Edmund Patch
Winslow.                          Nicholas Rouse
John Sanders
Andrew Weston[1]

1623 (Gorges) Sept.
"Six gentlemen and divers men to do his labor, and other men with their families."—Pratt.
A grandiose colonization project, fathered by the Council for New England, based on a grant of coast between Nahant and the mouth of the Charles River. They were therefore outside the grant.
[1] See Baxter's Levett, p. 126.

John Balch
Rev. Wm. Blaxton
John Bursley
Mr. Chapman[1]
Robert Gorges
Captain Hanson
William Jeffreys
? Thomas Lane
Samuel Maverick
Rev. William Morrell
Dr. Salisbury
? Capt. John Stone
Thomas Walford

## WINNESIMMET (CHELSEA, MASS.)

1625–34 Man and servants (also wife and stepson after 1628)    Samuel Maverick

## WINTER HARBOR (BIDDEFORD POOL)

(South side of the Saco River. Lewis and Bonython were later on the north side.)

1616–17 Possibly the next winter.    Richard Vines
1616–30    ? Morgan Howell
1618–19 Captain Rocroft put his mutinous crew ashore here but they went on to Monhegan where perhaps there was a greater store of food.

# Appendix C

# SOME AUTHORITIES

## I

Rosier's Relation of Waymouth's voyage to the Coast of Maine,
1605. Notes by Henry S. Burrage. Portland, Gorges Society, 1887.

> With a map showing Dr. Burrage's view of his explorations from Fisherman's Island to Boothbay Harbor, Wiscasset and Bath. See M. H. S. Proc., November, 1894, p. 182.

A Briefe and True Relation of Gosnold's Voyage. By John Brereton. G. Bishop, London, 1602.

> Text in Levermore's Forerunners.

A discourse of New-found-land. By Richard Whitbourne. London, 1623.

> Includes Capt. Edward Wynne's letters.

Westward ho for Avalon. By R. Whitbourne. London, 1622.

A Description of New England. By John Smith. London, 1616.
See M. H. Soc. Proc., November, 1894, p. 183.

New England's Trials [i. e., commercial ventures]. By John Smith. London, 1620. Also edited by C. Deane. Cambridge, 1873.

> The second edition, 1622, tells of 80 ships on the coast in 8 years, and describes Plymouth "begun by sixty weake men."

The Wilderness and the Indian. By C. C. Willoughby. Commonwealth History of Massachusetts. Vol. 1, Chapter VI, 1928.

History of Plymouth Plantation, 1620–1647. By William Bradford. 2 vols. Mass. Hist. Soc., 1912.

> Edited in masterly fashion by W. C. Ford.

Mourt's Relation. By Bradford and Winslow. London, 1622.
Also Boston, 1865.

> "A sort of journal."

Good newes from New-England. Written by E. W[inslow], London, 1624.

> From where Mourt ended down to September 10, 1623.

The Pilgrim Republic. By John A. Goodwin. Boston, 1888.
Good for personal detail. There is much of the background of the Pilgrims in Arber's Story of the Pilgrim Fathers, London, 1897.

The History of New England from 1630 to 1649. By John Winthrop. 2 vols. Boston, 1853.
A new critical edition is needed.

New England's Memoriall. By Nathaniel Morton. Cambridge, 1669. Edited by John Davis. Boston, 1826.
A non-religious history.

Wonder-Working Providence, 1628–1651. By Edward Johnson. London, 1654. Also New York, 1910.

Magnalia, 1620–1698. By Cotton Mather. London, 1702.

New-England's Prospect. By William Wood. London, 1639. Also Boston, Prince Society, 1865.

A Briefe Description of New England and the Severall Townes therein together with the Present Government thereof.
[By Samuel Maverick] Mass. Hist. Soc. Proc., October, 1884, p. 231.
A survey of the New England coast in 1660.

New England's Vindication. By Henry Gardener. Edited by Charles E. Banks, M.D. Portland, Maine, 1884.
Perhaps by Edward Godfrey.

Chronicles of the Pilgrim Fathers. By Alexander Young. Boston, 1897.

Forerunners and Competitors of the Pilgrims and Puritans. By C. H. Levermore. 2 vols. Brooklyn, 1912.
Useful texts.

The Founders of the Massachusetts Bay Colony. By Frank A. Gardner, M.D. Salem, 1908. From the Massachusetts Magazine.

The Founding of New England. By J. T. Adams. Boston, 1921.
Somewhat emancipated from the Puritan spell.

The Earliest Printed Sources of New England History, 1602–1629. By Justin Winsor. Mass. Hist. Soc. Proc., November, 1894, p. 181.

## II

Site of the Wessagusset Settlement. By C. F. Adams, Jr. Mass. Hist. Soc. Proc., November, 1891, p. 23.

"A Decliration of the Afaires of the Einglish People." By Phinehas Pratt. Mass. Hist. Soc. Coll., series iv, vol. 4, p. 475.
    A quaint story of colonial adventure.

Old Planters about Boston Harbor. By C. F. Adams, Jr. Mass. Hist. Soc. Proc., June, 1878, p. 194.
    A brilliant bit of reasoning.

Proceedings of the 250th Anniv. of the Permanent Settlement of Weymouth. By C. F. Adams, Jr. Boston, 1874.

Captain Wollaston, Humphrey Rasdell and Thomas Weston. By W. C. Ford. Mass. Hist. Soc. Proc., January, 1918, p. 219.

Thomas Morton of Merrymount. By C. E. Banks. Mass. Hist. Soc. Proc., December, 1924, p. 147; November, 1925, p. 92.
    New material.

New English Canaan of Thomas Morton. Amsterdam, 1637. Also Boston, Prince Society, 1883.
        But see B. F. DeCosta's "A few observations," N. Y., 1883.

## III

William Blackstone. By Rev. B. F. DeCosta. New York, 1880
    From the Churchman's point of view.

William Blaxton. By Thomas C. Amory. Bostonian Soc. Pub., vol. 1, no. 1, 1886.
    Now out of date.

Rev. William Blackstone. By John C. Crane. Worcester, 1896.

Lineage and History of William Blackstone. By J. W. Blackston. Frederic, Wis., 1907.

Mr. Blackstone's "excellent spring." By M. J. Canavan. Colon. Soc. of Mass. Pub., vol. 11, 1910.

History of Horncastle. By J. C. Walter. Horncastle, 1908.

Sketch of the History of Attleborough. By John Daggett. Boston, 1894.

History of Rehoboth. By L. Bliss, Jr. Boston, 1836.
        One of many local works by unappreciated historians.

Letters of Roger Williams, 1632–1682, edited by J. R. Bartlett. Providence, Narragansett Club, 1874.

Indenture of David Thomson and others. Mass. Hist. Soc. Proc., May, 1876, p. 358.

Maverick Family. By Mrs. Elizabeth French Bartlett. New Eng. Hist. Geneal. Reg., April, 1915, p. 146.

The Settlers about Boston Bay prior to 1630. By Lucie M. Gardner. Salem, 1910, pp. 12. From the Massachusetts Magazine.
> Includes Salem and Dorchester Colonists, 1629–1630.

## IV

The Landing at Cape Anne. By J. W. Thornton. Boston, 1854.
> An excellent pioneer work.

Bradford on a religious rival: Rev. John Lyford. By C. E. Banks. Mass. Hist. Soc. Proc., December, 1928.
> A fearless appeal to reason.

The Planters' Plea. By Rev. John White. London, 1630.

The "Old Planters" of Salem who were settled here before the arrival of Governor Endicott, in 1628. By George D. Phippen. Essex Inst. Hist. Coll., vol. 1, 1859, pp. 97, 145, 185; vol. 4, 1862, p. 127.
> An excellent work, with Roger Conant as the hero.

Richard Brackenbury's deposition, 1680–1. Essex Inst. Hist. Coll., vol. 1, 1859, p. 156.

History and Genealogy of the Conant Family. By F. O. Conant. Portland, 1887.

Old Planters Society. Publications, 1900–1910. 6 vols.

The Merchant Adventurers of England. A narrative of their settlement in Salem. By W. A. Pew. Privately printed, 1926.

Roger Conant, 1626, the leader of the old planters. By Frank A. Gardner. Salem, 1926.

## V

Religious Matters at the Piscataqua. By James De Normandie. Mass. Hist. Soc. Proc., May, 1902, p. 175.

Early Portsmouth History. By Ralph May. Boston, 1926.
> A good outline.

Transcripts of Original Documents in English Archives relating to
New Hampshire. By J. S. Jenness. N. Y., 1876. *Map.*
Documentary History of the State of Maine containing the Tre-
lawny Papers. Edited by J. P. Baxter, Portland, 1884. Coll.
Maine Hist. Soc., 2d series, vol. 3.
> An invaluable picture of a fishing enterprise in 1631.
The Beginnings of Colonial Maine, 1602–1658. By Henry S.
Burrage. Printed for the State, 1914.
> A detailed, scholarly work.
The Isles of Shoals. By J. S. Jenness. N. Y., 1873.
> An authoritative study.
Who' planted New Hampshire? By C. T. Libby. In The Granite
Monthly, October, 1922, pp. 364–368.
> Concerning Thomson and the Hiltons.

## VI

The Sagadahoc Colony. Notes by Rev. H. O. Thayer. Portland,
Maine, Gorges Society, 1892. Also see Mass. Hist. Soc.
Proc., vol. 18, 1880–81, p. 82 (De Costa).
Christopher Levett of York. By J. P. Baxter. Portland, Gorges
Society, 1893.
> An exhaustive monograph.
Pemaquid. In Maine Hist. Soc. Coll., 2d series, vol. 6 (1895),
pp. 53, 62.
The Fortunate Island of Monhegan. By C. F. Jenney. Worces-
ter, 1922. From vol. 31 of Amer. Antiq. Soc. Proc.
Damariscove. By Winfield Thompson. In New England Maga-
zine, September, 1894 (N. S., vol. XI), p. 34.
> The romance of the island.
Origin of the names Damariscove and Damariscotta not the same.
By Rev. H. O. Thayer. In Bath Independent, May 15,
1915. He upholds the Damerill theory.
> Lent me by Hon. W. D. Patterson.
Ancient Pemaquid. The Jamestown of New England. By H. O.
McCrillis. In New England Magazine, May, 1906 (vol.
XXXIV), p. 278.
History of the Discovery of Maine. By J. G. Kohl. (Doc. Hist.
of Maine, vol. 1, 1869).

# APPENDIX D

## EARLY NAMES

| | |
|---|---|
| Agamenticus | York, Maine |
| Bass River | Beverly, Mass. |
| Canada | Maine |
| Cape Manwagan | Boothbay, Maine |
| Cape Porpoise (Porpus) | Kennebunkport, Maine |
| Elizabeth Isle | Cuttyhunk, Mass. |
| Gorgeana | York, Maine |
| Great Island | Newcastle, N. H. |
| Hilton's Point | Dover, N. H. |
| Jeffreys Creek | Manchester, Mass. |
| Little Harbor | Odiorne's Point, N. H. |
| Merrymount | Wollaston, Mass. |
| Mishawum | Charlestown, Mass. |
| Natascot | Hull, Mass. |
| Naumkeag | Salem, Mass. |
| Nayantick | Westerly, R. I. |
| Newichawannock | Dover, N. H. |
| Northam | Dover, N. H. |
| Pasonagesset | Mt. Wollaston (Quincy, Mass.) |
| Pejepscot | Brunswick, Maine |
| Piscataqua | Kittery (Eliot, Berwick) |
| Popham Beach | Phipsburg, Maine |
| Quack | Portland, Maine |
| Savage Rock | Cape Neddick, York |
| Salvages | Rocks off Cape Ann |

| | |
|---|---|
| Shawmut | Boston, Mass. |
| Strawberry Bank | Portsmouth, N. H. |
| Study Hill | Lonsdale village in the town of Cumberland, R. I. |
| Three Turks Heads | York, Maine. Also rocks off Cape Ann |
| Wessagusset | Weymouth, Mass. |
| Winnesimmet | Chelsea, Mass. |
| Winter Harbor | Biddeford Pool, Maine |

# INDEX

CPSIA information can be obtained at www.ICGtesting.com
Printed in the USA
BVOW041735160812

298073BV00005/P